MW01170992

IF ONLY she...

IF
ONLY
she...

DIANE HARTH

LUMINARE PRESS
WWW.LUMINAREPRESS.COM

IF ONLY she…
Copyright © 2024 by Diane Harth

Printed in the United States of America

Luminare Press
442 Charnelton St.
Eugene, OR 97401
www.luminarepress.com

LCCN: 2024914890
ISBN: 979-8-88679-640-7

For my granddaughters,
Tricia, Kendall, Ellie, and Bridget.

There will come a time in your lives when
you will wonder about your ancestors.
I have written this memoir for all of you.

This is my story.

With that in mind, I also dedicate this memoir
to my paternal grandmother, Josephine
and great grandmother, Rose.

My strength and resilience comes from them.

FORETHOUGHT

If only we were all loved. If only we all had a voice that could be expressed without criticism or consequences. If only we were all accepted for who we are and not who others want us to be or believe we should be. Could we thrive by being silent, by being an outcast, by being a scapegoat, by being invisible? What would it be like to not be supported, encouraged, and recognized for who you are?

This is my story.

AUTHOR'S NOTE

This book is a memoir reflecting my relationship with my biological family and how that shaped my life. It is based on my experiences and my perceptions. My analysis of myself and my mother was taken from decades of therapy and how I perceived the world. Some of the names have been changed to maintain privacy for certain individuals.

Chapter 1

TRAUMA

I do not remember all the details of the incident, only the ones that really count. It was sometime in the early to mid-sixties, which would make me about eight or nine years old. Growing up we did not go into Manhattan much, but there was a time when my parents took us to Radio City Music Hall to see the Christmas show. My mother was always impressed with the Rockettes, enthralled with how they danced. Every Thanksgiving we would watch the Macy's Thanksgiving Day parade on TV, and when the Rockettes came on, she would stop cooking our turkey dinner and come in and watch them dance. And for this old-fashioned Sicilian to leave the stove and stop cooking…this was a big deal. My mother could never be interrupted and taken away from her "wifely" chores.

The kick line was most impressive to her. The Rockettes were arranged in size order. The tallest in the middle, center of attention, with the height of the women sloping down, so that the shortest women were at the ends of the line. The straight lines, the high kicks, all in sync and no one out of step. How do they do that so perfectly? She would stand halfway in the living room and halfway in the kitchen, one eye on the TV and the other on the pot. Like something out of *The Exorcist* movie. She always said she had eyes in the back of her head; as a child, I thought she was able to rotate her head in a complete circle. Although I had never seen her do that, it was the only explanation as to why nothing got past her. I was terrified of my mother. To me, she was a very scary person.

I know now that it was her own imperfect self and her need to be perfect—that is why she gravitated toward these women, the Rockettes, who she thought were flawless. An image she strived for but could never achieve on her own. The closest to perfection she was able to attain was her compulsive investment in keeping her house clean. She employed a complete armory of tools to engage in this undertaking. Her arsenal for the war against dirt included the dustpan, the vacuum cleaner, the dust rag, and her almighty favorite, Clorox. My mother's house was as sterilized as an operating room in a hospital. My analyst once said to me, "The next house I buy will be your mother's." I do not know anyone who has bought a house that was sparkling clean. Cleanliness was perceived as a reflection of my mother, and she didn't want anyone to think less of her.

This standard of excellence, and a standard that she unconsciously wanted her children to measure up to, was apparent in her denial of who her children really were. I say unconsciously because there was never any outward pressure on us to be perfect. I do not remember pressure to get good grades or being punished for a bad report card. There was never pressure to "be the best we could be" or any discussions about going to college, especially for me and my sister. The pressure for perfection only became apparent if something was a reflection on her—no one needed to know about our grades. Interestingly, her need for perfection had its limitations. Clearly, when it came to parenting, she was completely stunted.

I remember being outside of Radio City on the street. It was a nice day, clear skies, but also cold. Global warming had not yet emerged its "hot head" into the political arena. The show was over and we were preparing for the ride home to New Jersey. We were standing in front of Radio City. My memory is not that clear, and I'm not sure if this is due to trauma or my age. I suspect it is more trauma than age since I remember some specific aspects of the incident. The brain has the capacity in the midst of a traumatic event to block out certain details. The brain protects you from the overwhelming terror of the traumatic event. And I believe that is why my memory is spotty pertaining to my family's reactions. I will tell you the "incident" was never discussed, as my parents were not big on conversations or emotions. I also believe, if it had been discussed, it might have reflected poorly on my mother. Therefore, the silence prevailed!

I do not remember the atmosphere of NYC, seeing homeless people or the smell of garbage on the curb. I have no recollection of the noise of the city; the horns honking, police sirens, or ambulances speeding by. I am unsure if there were lots of people on the street, pushing their way through the densely populated holiday streets of the city, that I know exist today. But the following is what I do remember.

My sister, Trish, was four years older than me, and my brother, Dominic, was fourteen months older. My siblings were standing next to my parents, as was I, when a man grabbed me and pulled me away from them. He wasn't much taller than me, had kind of a scruffy beard, a rather elongated face, and was dark-skinned. There were no words spoken between the two of us. It happened so quickly. He was not running with me and did not physically hurt me. It was like taking a stroll in the park, easy, not tense, as if I was walking down the street holding hands with a relative. I am sure, at the time, I was unable to comprehend what was transpiring. I was always taught to respect my elders so there was no resistance, no talking back. I did not scream. I did not cry. I just went along with him. Stranger danger was not a "thing" back then. My passivity may be suggestive of a dissociative state, in which one is disconnected from thoughts, feelings, memories, or a sense of identity. This could help to explain my memory lapse.

He held my left hand, and I remember looking back at my parents and my siblings with my right arm extended toward them as if to say: "Please help me! What is going on? Was this planned? Was this your idea?" I have no recollection of my family panicking. I heard nothing. My life was in slow motion. The pace of the city had slowed down like a record going from seventy-eight to forty-five to thirty-three rpm's. What I do recall was the four of them standing there looking back at me, with flat affect. In retrospect, could they have been saying, "That is one less problem we have to worry about"? I am sure I must have felt overlooked at that point. I know it was only a matter of seconds before my father retrieved me and I was reunited with my family. However, it seemed as if it took a long time for him to rescue me.

I have always wondered if my mother was thinking, "Thank God *you* two are safe," referring to my siblings. Were they really going to let me leave? Were my nightmares, which had started years before, coming true? I had never felt safe or protected by my parents, and now this "incident" was evidence that my anxiety and fears were valid.

As I recall these events, the events which happened over sixty-something years ago, I am finally able to let out my emotions and actually allow myself to feel sorry for myself. I am able to cry and feel the emotion of being alone. I'm able to feel the pain. These emotions were so forbidden in my biological family. The unconscious has now become conscious.

The feeling of being unwanted and unloved followed me for decades. The "incident" validated my unconscious, anticipatory apprehensive anxiety about not feeling safe in my own family. Not feeling that my mother was ever invested in my well-being. A feeling of not belonging and a feeling of being overlooked and forgotten. I can say that it was probably no more than a few minutes, or maybe seconds, before my father retrieved me from this man. However, to me, experiencing the trauma of the event made it seem endless.

That sense of not belonging and not being loved by my parents has followed me throughout my life. I never had a lot of friends, and my relationships never lasted long. If my own parents didn't love me, how could anyone else love me? It was not just about love; it was more about my parents not liking me and making me the scapegoat for all their problems. For the world's problems. For example, the Vietnam War was my fault, in case anyone is still looking for an answer to the war. I was blamed for everything. At least that was my perception, and one's feelings and perceptions can be more powerful, at times, than reality.

Liking someone is more important than loving someone. A child knows when someone likes them, but when it comes to family, one always assumes they love you. Love is not just a feeling, it is an action that takes work. Therefore, how could one love someone whom one does not like? What would it be like to be the recipient of that? To be the recipient would be very confusing. I was the recipient of possibly being loved but knowing I was not liked. This perception had an effect on all of my future relationships. It leads to bewildering questions. Am I likable? Am I loveable?

Decades later I discussed this in therapy and my therapist suggested I speak to my family about the incident. I took his advice and asked Dominic if he remembered what happened on that day. I wanted to know what my family's reaction was. He immediately recalled the event and said that my mother was screaming at my father to get me. I have no memory of my mother screaming. I must have dissociated and blocked it out. I guess it was my father's job to retrieve me, as gender roles were very specific back then. My other thought was that she possibly was afraid, herself, to confront the man. I, unfortunately, cannot accept that rationale. I would sacrifice my life for my children. Would my mother have behaved the same way if it was one of my siblings? I wonder if it was my sister who had been taken, would my mother have just stood there? Sixty years later, I can justify these questions based on my conscious and unconscious feelings and decades of therapy. I now can see my family in a more objective way.

What kind of environment could create such fear, terror, and anxiety in a child that sixty years later, the emotional scars are still palpable and able to be triggered, simply by writing a description of an event from the past? These emotions are able to surface today because of the relationship I am in now. A relationship full of trust that allows for such emotions to be expressed and openly discussed.

I always wondered what my mother might have gone through seeing her child pulled away by a stranger, my mother who was a ball of anxiety. I wonder how this "incident" affected her, if at all. Was she paralyzed with fear? Did she dissociate? Was she so stricken with terror that she became immobilized? Did this event have any effect on her at all? Did she just bury it deep inside of her psyche, in that little black box to which no key existed to unleash those emotionally hidden demons? Her thoughts locked and boundless, in the dark depths of her bottomless reservoir that kept all her secrets? I will never know.

Knowing my mother, she probably made the incident about herself. I can hear her telling her sisters: "You cannot believe what happened to me today," as everything was always about my mother. She was unable to really listen to anyone else. I have lived a lifetime of talking to my mother on the phone and she would inquire about how I was doing, then literally two minutes into the conversation she would say: "I don't mean to interrupt or cut you off, but...", and she would proceed to tell me what's going on in her life.

Decades later, I would be triggered by another Radio City event. It was not as traumatic, but it triggered me, and I was more aware of the sensation that perforated my inner core. Again, it was quick. The only harm to me was to my psyche.

When my kids were in grade school, there was a class trip to Radio City to see the Christmas show. Both my husband and I attended the class trip. After the show, I turned to my husband and said, "I have to use the bathroom, please wait for me." Unfortunately, when I was in the bathroom, the ushers demanded that everyone leave the auditorium immediately. When I came out of the bathroom, no one was there. The ushers instructed me to leave through another door and not the main entrance that I originally came through, which led me out to an unfamiliar street. I did not see the school bus or my husband. Then the thoughts started to emerge. I did not trust that my husband would come find me. I did not trust that the bus would wait for me and it would leave. I thought to myself "How am I going to get home?" I was in complete distress and became confused. The adrenaline that raged through my body was crushing, and I started to shake. I started walking to find the front entrance, and as I was walking, I saw my husband walking toward me. I remember yelling at him and letting out the fear and the rage I felt inside of me. What seemed like a long time was, again, only a few minutes. But I was panicked and seeing him offered me no sense of relief because, like with my mother, I did not feel safe.

Growing up, it was the silence, the unspoken words that were abusive to me. There was no physical abuse aside from, infrequently, being hit with a strap by my father. One might expect this to be a possible explanation for the nightmares and feeling unwanted. It was more about the emotional wasteland that I experienced that was so devastating as to be able to induce a lifelong level of hypervigilance and anxiety for this child! This dissociative use of the phrase "this child" just underscores the severity of the neglect I endured. Silencing someone, always dismissing their feelings and experiences, in addition to feeling personally dismissed, is traumatic. Writing has allowed me to express it. Writing has allowed me to better understand the past in more depth. It has been a therapeutic experience.

Trauma is an interesting emotional response to an incident. It is not something that disappears. It is always with you. Once the trauma is processed and accepted, it no longer controls you, and you can live with it more comfortably. But it never completely leaves you. The impact of these events has stayed with me forever on many levels. I try to avoid the city as much as I can. My hypervigilance lingers within me. I'm always three steps ahead of a possible tragedy, with a plan in mind.

Chapter 2

TRUST

It was dark. It was the middle of a winter's night. I was snuggled in my bed with the blankets up around my neck and my arms intertwined, curled up like a pretzel. My knees were bent and up against my stomach; in the fetal position. Although my sister was in the bed next to me, I still felt very much alone. As I lay awake in my bed, as I had many nights before, the nightly fear once again continued to inundate my entire being. Was it going to happen again? Would I survive this time? Would anyone hear my screams? Would anyone come to rescue me?

I heard the rattling of the door. I started to shake. My body began to quiver. It was dark, there were no night lights in my bedroom. I got out of my bed, barefoot and cold. I hoped that he would not find me again, that he would not catch me again, that I would survive another night. I am suddenly alone in a place that I do not recognize. I started to run. I ran for my life.

There was a man chasing me. This man was a stranger, but all I was focused on was finding a place to hide. I had to escape. I started to pick up the pace and my tiny feet were moving as fast as they could. I was small, a young child, and had the advantage of escaping, hiding in small spaces, crevices, in the hope that I would not be found. But I knew how this would end because I had never escaped in the past. I was always found. I was shivering, and I was unaware if this was from fright or the cold of not being in bed on this wintery night.

I hid and hoped he would not find me again. Unfortunately, I saw his shadow. He found me. He caught me. He stabbed me in the back, and I could feel my back arching as the knife was embedded deep within me. I could feel the warmth of my blood trickling down my body. I started to scream. No one heard me. No one came to help me. And then my body relaxed, and I, once again, rescued myself. I felt relieved. I woke up.

These nightmares were almost a nightly occurrence that continued for decades, way into adulthood. I was very young when the nightmares began, maybe four years old. I have no recollection of ever telling my parents about these nightmares. What I find interesting is that even at a young age, I realized my parents would not have been concerned about my nightmares.

The healthier I became as a result of therapy, the more I noticed the content of my nightmares changed. The nightmares morphed into something different. I was able to escape the man who was chasing me and stabbing me. I was no longer caught by this man who was going to annihilate me. The nightmares changed at a point when my anxiety and anger decreased. They changed when I started to have more trust in the world. Additionally, the nightmares ended when I divorced the father of my children, as he had several behavioral traits that my mother had.

A young child doesn't always have the capacity to verbalize feelings or even recognize what those feelings are about. But my nightmares came from a feeling that I was unable to rely on and trust that my parents would emotionally care for and support me. Dreams are a way of suppressing emotion. In my case the brain was protecting me from the reality of trauma. That trauma of knowing my parents' true feelings about me. I was unwanted.

Recurring dreams/nightmares can be a sign of anxiety. It is difficult for me to acknowledge how old I was when I became aware that I was unwanted. I believe I experienced the feeling of not being wanted very early on. The man in my nightmare could have been either my mother or my father, as dreams are always camouflaged. The nightmare was not far from the truth, as I became consciously aware of this fact many years later. I was alone in my family forever. I was anxious, fearful, and mistrusting of everyone. I often wonder if the stabbing was my mother's desire to abort me. This nightmare had lasting effects on me. Even today, my initial response when the power goes out and I am in the dark is to panic.

For as long as I could remember, I experienced a relationship with my parents in which I did not feel safe and protected. I had no sense of trust in the universe. Failure to develop trust can result in fear and the belief that the world is inconsistent and unpredictable. When caregivers provide reliability, care, and affection, one develops a sense of trust.

In the absence of this, I felt there was nothing I could trust. This led to decades of dysfunctional relationships, anger, and anxiety. It left me feeling that the world is unsafe and no one could ever be trusted. A feeling of emptiness.

Chapter 3

INTERGENERATIONAL TRAUMA: MY MOTHER'S TRAUMA

In my professional experience as a clinical social worker, many clients have questioned the importance of taking a family history. Many felt that the past had nothing to do with the present. Trauma, almost always, is passed down from generation to generation, and in most cases, unintentionally, because people can be unaware of their own trauma. I, therefore, feel obligated to explore my family's history in order to determine why and how my parents were unable to nurture me in an environment with love and trust.

Intergenerational trauma is defined as the result of having ancestors who have experienced distressing or oppressive events, of which the emotional and behavioral reactions ripple through generations of family members and dramatically affect the next generation.

It is quite difficult to describe what my mother's original trauma was, primarily because she never spoke about her childhood. I can only hypothesize what the original trauma was and what her childhood could have been like based on just two incidents that I am aware of, one of which I was only told about after her death.

Her trauma became etched in her psyche, from which she was unable to escape. Her feelings of despair lingered throughout her lifetime. This trauma became the foundation of how she functioned and processed her dilemmas and emotions throughout her life. I suspect that her negative outlook on life and how she attempted to raise her children were a reflection of this original trauma.

I would like to quote Mary Trump, a clinical psychologist who describes trauma in her book, *The Reckoning*. "Trauma can be quiet and slow, occurring over time in a tense drama of sameness, hopelessness and unbearable isolation, loneliness and helplessness. We fail to recognize trauma while being traumatized. To be traumatized is to be initiated into a world without trust." This was not only my mother's life but my life as well. The only difference between us is that my mother "lived" under its spell while I overcame it through the intervention of therapy. My mother existed as a victim.

To explore the genesis of my mother's trauma, I think it would be helpful to describe my maternal grandparents. My mother's parents immigrated to the States, Brooklyn, NY, from Sicily, about a year after they honeymooned in the States. My grandfather was in construction and my grandmother was a "stay-at-home mom," caring for her six daughters and "keeping house." In a recent conversation I had with my cousin Dennis, I found out that my grandmother worked as a seamstress, which helped supplement the family income. Another piece of the puzzle! I now understand where my mother got her talent for making clothes, as she made almost all of my clothes.

I felt like I truly loved my maternal grandmother, but in retrospect, I have no recollection of ever being close to her or having a conversation with her. This is an example of an early lack of intimacy, which most likely was present between her and her daughters. I wonder if it was because there were too many grandchildren and too much activity going on when I did see her. Having six daughters and nineteen grandchildren can be a handful. I am surprised she did not leave the house when we all visited. But now I understand why I felt lost in the shuffle. There was rarely, if ever, an opportunity to be alone with her to have that experience of intimacy. The opportunity to connect with her did not present itself.

When the family gathered at her house on Sunday for macaroni and meatballs, we would not be there all at once, just a few aunts and cousins at a time. I suppose she alternated Sundays with her daughters, so it didn't become too overwhelming for her. After all, feeding nineteen grandkids, six daughters, and their spouses, would call for a catering hall, not the basement of a small house in Brooklyn.

Sunday dinner in the basement! It was a basement with the small windows near the ceiling looking out onto the driveway. The room was very large with a very long table to fit everyone. There was a full kitchen, stove, sink, and refrigerator, but no dishwasher, as my aunts were the dishwashers. The moment you walked down into the basement, you could feel the steam rising from the pot of hot water, macaroni sitting on the counter, waiting for the pot to boil and to be poured into the macaroni pot. That smell, the sweet aroma of the gravy and meatballs, was mesmerizing. And if you were there early enough, before everyone else arrived, you got to dip the Italian bread into the pot of gravy. As you walked down the stairs, your salivary glands became a waterfall inside your mouth, and you could actually feel the sensation on your tongue sending wonderful messages to your brain. You were drawn into the scent of meatballs frying in the hot oil and getting yelled at to move away from the stove as the splatter of hot oil would always burn someone. The sweet smell of tomato sauce, garlic, onions, oregano, parsley, and basil mixed in with pork and chop meat in the gravy gave me a sense of calmness and a feeling of warmth. The aroma can only be described through emotions, mainly calmness and a feeling of being home. Maybe that was what gave me the sense of intimacy and the illusion of feeling close to my grandmother.

The adults sat at the table nearest the stairway and the oven; the kids sat at the other end closer to the wine cellar. My cousins always talked about the seating arrangements for Sunday dinner. I, myself, was never tuned into that, maybe because I always felt lost in the shuffle or maybe I never cared too much about where I sat. Where you sat was based on how grandma ranked you in that particular week. The closer to the wine cellar, the lower you ranked. I remember being somewhere in the middle most times.

It was organized chaos. You couldn't hear yourself think between the laughter, cousins fighting and the parents always yelling. Yelling to be able to be heard or just plain yelling at each other. Yelling, in my Italian family, was part of the culture. What I remember the most at the dinner table was hearing the following—"What's a matta, you not hungry, you too skinny"—and another ladle full of macaroni was dumped on your plate whether you wanted it or not. Eating was a sign of being healthy, that everything was in good working order. It was also the genesis of eating disorders. If you're not eating, something was very much wrong, and that message was ingrained in me forever. In my family, food was a way of showing love. There was no hugging or kissing and significant communication was minimal at best. We swam in an intimacy of gravy.

My mother's house was her domain; however, there was a mystery about it. There are an enormous amount of details that are missing from her life. My mother never spoke about her childhood, and I mean never. I know little to nothing about what went on in her childhood home. I do not know if there was any substantial communication that took place in her house, but in retrospect, I would have to think there was not. I conclude this, primarily, because there was no communication that went on in my house growing up. There was only superficial communication, like the weather and if there was traffic on the roads. There were no emotions expressed, no nothing. It was a totally barren landscape. A barren landscape that could have been cultivated but never was.

Diane Harth

I believe my mother suffered a great deal of trauma as a child. She had five sisters and grew up during the Great Depression. It must have been extremely difficult for all six of them, because none of my aunts, to my knowledge, ever discussed their childhoods with their own children. In the past, I asked several of my cousins if their mothers ever spoke about their childhood, and it seems that no one knows any details about their own mother's upbringing. This absence of information compounds the aura of mystery. There were only superficial stories, such as going out on dates together or sibling rivalries. No talk about famine or the difficulties endured during the Depression. It is typical for most people not to want to discuss their own personal trauma.

When my mom passed away in 2016, my son asked my aunt to describe what life was like when she was growing up in Brooklyn. She told him a story that I had never heard. Things were so bad during the Depression that one time all six of the sisters shared a single orange while sitting in front of an open oven to keep warm. They ate the pulp and put the leftover rind of the orange on the oven rack to fill the room with the aroma. My son said that my aunt spoke more about the smell than the taste. Olfactory memory is distinctively powerful and probably the scent of the orange gave the house a sense of warmth and comfort and, possibly more importantly, a feeling of safety. When my son disclosed this to me, I immediately felt numb and disbelief. It was difficult to comprehend the level of poverty and deprivation they suffered. Why was my mother unable to discuss this? Possibly because she was devastatingly shamed by something that was not caused by her or anything that her parents did. Everyone was suffering the same deprivation of basic needs. But my mother was extremely vain and ashamed of her background. I have to assume that this was due to living in poverty and the options that she felt were unavailable for her in her life. I do not know, and can only imagine, what my grandparents' attitude regarding the Great Depression was and what messages were given to the children either consciously or unconsciously. I do not know how my mother and my aunts were made to feel. Were they meant to feel ambivalently grateful or guilty for what little they had and shame for what they didn't have? All I know is that it was a taboo topic suggesting shame and guilt.

My mother's upbringing affected how she raised her own children and how she related to them, passing on a pattern of neglect that employed shame and guilt and silence. By passing on this oppressive legacy to her children, she took away our sense of self-empowerment and created a feeling of lack of control over our own lives. This gave us the perception of impotence, which undermined our capacity for individuation and developing a sense of independence. This is the intergenerational trauma.

The only story my mother ever told me as a child was the following. My mother and her older sister were forced to drop out of school in order to help support the family; my mother, after the eighth grade, and my aunt in high school. It was quite typical for children to leave school during this time. There were also many schools that closed because the maintenance of keeping the schools open was nearly impossible to sustain. There was little money to pay for utilities. My mother left school and worked in a factory. The fascinating piece of this was I also worked in a factory as a teenager.

My mother said this decision, made by her mother for her, was the most traumatic event in her life. My mom said she loved school and always wanted to continue her education. But it was stolen from her! I can only imagine my mother's level of disappointment and depression that had enveloped her entire being; what it was like being an adolescent one day and an adult the next to help support the family. For my mother, there was no gathering at a friend's house after school or hanging out on the street corner, going for an ice cream soda at the local drug store, or roller-skating at the local rink; there was only work. What were once streets filled with people laughing, going to the movies, and basically having fun were now at a minimum. The lines that people were waiting on were no longer for the movies but lines waiting for bread. A line with women cradling their babies as toddlers held onto their mother's legs, waiting for any kind of food to feed their hungry children. What she saw were people walking aimlessly, roaming, confused, looking desperate, distressed, and pained. She watched people steal food and beg for food to avoid starvation. People gathered at soup kitchens, as this was their only source of nourishment. She witnessed the panic at local savings and loan banks as people tried to withdraw their money and were told there was no money left in their bank accounts. Their only relief was listening to the radio. Music and dancing were sources of fun, and everyone knew how to jitterbug back then.

This intergenerational trauma was directly passed down to me by my mother, forcing me to go out to work as soon as I was of age and taking half my paycheck for herself. This is a very good working hypothesis for why my mother was so controlling; she could not control anything. If your life is out of control, your option is to try to control everything with impunity. Impunity especially directed toward me, because I was not a planned birth. Therefore, her decision to give birth to me was out of her control, or at least she felt that she had no choice but to continue with the pregnancy. The domain of her control was inside the house in terms of cooking and cleaning. The only thing she felt she could control was keeping the house clean, which became a compulsion. And her compulsion alleviated her anxiety. Her anxiety was prompted by her having a lack of control in her life. My mother was in denial of her anxiety, and her anxiety was like a tsunami most of the time. A tsunami that washed over her, dragging her children with her into the ocean's ebb, the way the ocean recedes into the darkness, into the abyss of her own neurosis.

Decades later, my aunt—my mother's older sister—told me that she and my mom made a pact to never let this happen to their four younger sisters, thereby, allowing them to complete their high school education. My mother was so ashamed and embarrassed about her life and the hardships she encountered that she never spoke about her childhood to anyone. She would always say: "I'm a very private person." The only thing she ever disclosed to me was this trauma about her lack of education.

The outside world never saw the shame and pain my mother endured during her childhood. She would put on a façade that everything was wonderful. Her nieces and nephews always had positive feelings for her, as I did for my aunts. But secrets were a big thing in her family and the six sisters *never* talked about their childhood hardships. This might have been the glue that solidified their relationship. They were bonded by tragedy, whatever that tragedy was, beyond what's known. A true secret, the mystery, always lurking below the surface, capable of making an appearance at any inappropriate moment. The shame and anxiety prevented them from ever coming to the surface.

And those secrets continued when my mother started her own family. She did not know how to communicate with my father or her children. She did not know how to soothe anyone with her words. It was just "Get over it." She was unable to show positive emotions. Only anger and anxiety. What I learned from that was that my only options were to be angry or anxious. This is a good example of how trauma gets passed from one generation to the next.

The secrets though were one thing, but gossip took a completely different turn. The sisters would all gossip among themselves, and the biggest joke was "Don't tell anyone *but…*" Everyone knew everything about everyone and simultaneously believed that they were the holder of all the information. Being the holder of secrets, or information, gave them the ability to have power and control over each other, as well as their own levels of anxiety. The only way my mother kept a secret was if at some point it was a reflection of her, if it embarrassed her.

But she always kept my siblings' secrets. Apparently, I did not hold the same status as my siblings. She always divulged my secrets to everyone and anyone. I was the one who was most afraid of her and the one who needed the most to be loved and accepted by her. And because my mother knew I was the one most afraid of her, she knew there would be no consequences for divulging my confidences that I shared with her when I was young. When someone needs to be loved and accepted by another, loyalty to that person is undying, especially if there are occasional crumbs thrown at you to maintain that loyalty. The psychological explanation for this persistence of loyalty is referred to as intermittent reinforcement. This occasional crumb allows for that loyalty and connection to persist. This is what explains a gambler's addiction. Every now and then they win, reinforcing their desire to continue to bet.

My mother also knew that I was the only one who was very independent, which could benefit her later on in life. In her mind, I was the one who could take care of her in her old age. The older I got, the more I was aware of this assumption on her part, and I knew that I would *never* physically take care of her. My independence was for my own survival and emotional well-being.

But I "respected" her out of fear. Fear is not an emotion that teaches respect. It simply creates a façade. The fear was never knowing how she was going to react and how it was going to be turned around on me. Do I express all my thoughts and feelings to her at once or just edit them? How do I get rid of the butterflies in my stomach to approach her? How will she use it against me and embarrass me in front of others? Were there any benefits to disclosing to her what was going on in my life? Obviously not because I couldn't trust her. And this distrust culminated in a lifetime characteristic for which I spent decades in treatment to be able to accept that everyone is not like my mother. I learned how not to trust from my mother.

The secrets, I guess, came from my mother having five sisters and living in an era of poverty. There was no privacy. There was no room for anyone to express their emotions, and my mother's emotions were displaced by her anxiety. It's possible that any emotional issues that my siblings and I experienced growing up were triggers for my mother. Her lack of coping skills and displaced emotions were manifested by projecting all her insecurities onto her children. For example, my mother was terrified of life and saw the world as a very unsafe place. My sister, Trish, had social anxiety when out in public; however, she felt insulated from her anxiety when surrounded by family and cousins. She was afraid to drive, to meet new people, and to challenge herself with new experiences. Dominic's anxiety manifested itself in doing the opposite. He needed to be surrounded by lots of people and needed to have lots of friends. But he needed to be liked. His defense mechanism was joking. As for me, I suffered with anxiety throughout my life and had the ability to cut off people who did me wrong in a heart-beat, which was not a good coping mechanism. I would shut the door immediately before seeing that there could be other possibilities as to why the person behaved the way they did. This was my attachment issue—if something goes wrong, dump them before they dump you because it was less painful in the moment. After decades of therapy, I've learned to take a step back and think before I act. I'm much less impulsive today.

And then there was my grandfather. I wish I had the experience of really knowing my maternal grandfather. My life was surrounded by women and women who suffered emotionally throughout their lives. I only had one grandfather. I never knew my paternal grandfather. Unfortunately, I was quite young when my maternal grandfather died. I vaguely remember what he looked like. Not a very tall man, with a long face. That is my memory of him. He made his own wine in the cellar, which my parents referred to as "Guinea Red." One day he told my grandmother he was going down to the cellar. My grandmother said she had a funny feeling something bad was going to happen (these feelings happen to be a Sicilian trait). She went downstairs and found him dead on the floor. I was five years old at the time, and it was my first introduction to death. It was the first time I ever saw a dead person. I do remember crying and being very emotional at his funeral. Like most cultures, funerals take on their own dynamic. When I was growing up in this Italian household, it was who could cry and wail the loudest at a funeral. Not quite sure if that meant the loudest was the one who loved the deceased the most or what. But that's what it was.

Walking up to the casket, I felt all the butterflies in my stomach, emotionally confused, wanting to see him and wanting to run out of the room both at the same time. I remember kneeling by the coffin. I had some anxiety about seeing my grandpa lying in a bed of what looked like very cushy pillows, like sleeping on a cloud surrounded by this wooden container. Maybe the cushy pillows were a metaphor for him rising up to heaven, up in the clouds. I had no idea what to expect. I was unable to grasp the idea of being dead, never coming back; he looked like he was just sleeping. This is all that I remember. An overwhelming sense of anxiety with no one to explain it to me.

Unfortunately, death, pregnancy (I remember my aunts being pregnant and not understanding any of it), and all the important issues that life brings to you were never discussed in my house. No comfort, no explanation, no talking. There was no "Grandpa loved you," no processing of thoughts or feelings. Just suck it up and move on.

My mother was already planting the seeds for my success as a clinical social worker, and neither of us knew it. My childhood experiences significantly determined my future; I was always that child who needed to know everything, wanted to talk, needed to talk. This was how I controlled my own anxiety. When you're kept in the dark, you have no idea what to expect, and the dark, for me, was terrifying because of my nightmares. The nightmares are a symptom of intergenerational trauma. I hated surprises. Surprises were something that I was unable to control and provoked anxiety. I always had to be three steps ahead of everything. Having a plan meant that I was going to be OK. I would survive. Having a plan decreased my anxiety. It was a comfort to me. Later on in life, I realized that talking, listening, and planning were essential skills needed to be a successful clinical social worker.

After my grandfather's death, my grandmother wore black for decades to come. It was the Italian custom. She wasn't alone, as my aunt and uncle continued to live with her and care for her well into her old age. She died in 1988 while in a nursing home suffering from Alzheimer's. My mother never showed her emotions when her mom died. I never saw her cry; she never visibly broke down. She appeared emotionless. But I was unaware of what she did privately. This is how I learned to deal with death…you don't. The only time I saw my mother cry was when my sister died. But again, there was no talking, no processing of feelings. Denial was her defense mechanism. My mother was inept when it came to handling her own emotions. Emotions were just too painful for her, and she had no coping skills to manage her pain. Her emotional pain was an unattended open wound, which was consistently displaced onto me. This was the essence of my life that defined me for decades. That trauma of knowing my parents' true feelings about me. I was unwanted.

Chapter 4

AND THEN THERE'S MY DAD

The ambience in my father's house growing up was much different from the atmosphere in my mother's house. Although I have much more information regarding my dad's childhood, there are some questions as to why his behavior appeared inconsistent at times. He vacillated between being strong and scary and weak and mild-mannered. I suspect this may be due to the number of family members he was surrounded by in his house who all had many different perspectives and outlooks on life. Another theory to explain his inconsistency might be that he may not have been exposed to a woman like my mother ever before. Looking at my father's history can answer some questions but not all questions.

His parents immigrated to the States, Brooklyn, NY, from Naples, in the early 1920s, before he was born. My grandfather was a musician and my grandmother and great-grandmother were midwives. My dad's father passed when he was somewhere between two and four years old. Coincidentally, my children's paternal grandfather also died when their father was four. My dad had an older sister and a younger brother. He was the middle child. My grandmother had another pregnancy; however, the child was either mis-carried or a stillbirth.

My dad told me that my grandfather was a very gener-ous man. He financially helped a lot of people. Unfortu-nately, when he died, so did the loans. The loans were never paid back to my grandmother; the people that my grand-father helped ghosted my grandmother. My grandmother never saw any of that money again. However, I never had the feeling they were left financially destitute.

My grandmother was not alone. She lived in an apart-ment building that was occupied by her siblings, cousins, and her mother. My father had many male role models and people to look up to. He was cared for and loved, and I would describe my dad's childhood as good, despite the Great Depression.

The atmosphere surrounding my dad's family was a bit different from my mom's family. I can honestly say it was a much more relaxed environment. It just seemed like noth-ing was much of a big deal, which appeared not to be the case in my mother's family. My mother's family was a "bit" more tense and anxious. My dad said his house was filled with laughter, fun, and what I would describe as rowdiness, given the number of people who came in and out of his house on a daily basis. There seemed to be much more of an open-door policy in which people would just stop over with no invitation and be warmly welcomed. The phrase I often heard in my dad's family when someone stopped over was "Put the pot up," meaning boil the water for the macaroni.

He talked about his Catholic education and how he

became "turned off" by the church, an institution that forever turned him away from his religion, never going into any detail. I can surmise growing up Italian along with the rigidity of the Catholic Church was too oppressive for him. Between these two "cultures," I'm sure there wasn't much room for freedom of expression. I believe his joy was from playing stickball in the street and working hard, as that was what he frequently talked about.

My dad was very smart. He was offered a scholarship to attend college in Italy when he graduated from high school but turned it down despite the family's encouragement. He felt he needed to stay home and help to financially support his mother. I do not have the sense that my dad's family was as financially destitute as my mom's family; however, I am sure it was not easy. I do not believe there were any "orange" issues in their household. However, family ties were very strong for my father back then, and I'm sure that was his incentive not to attend college in Italy. Had he gone to college, he most likely would not have served in the military, which was very important to him. He said he would count down the days until he was drafted. To him it was an honor to serve. And he did serve. He was in the army during WWII. He served on a ship, never on land, providing supplies for the war effort.

I only know one story about his time in the service. One day when he was on the ship, he spotted another ship close by. He told a buddy of his that the other ship was going to crash into their ship. Evidently my dad was tuned into the course the other ship was taking; the direction of the bow and how the waves were rolling toward his ship. As the ship sailed closer, time seemed to stop; he was unable to identify what should be done first. I don't know if the captain was notified or if he was aware of the upcoming tragedy that was about to strike. I can picture the men scrambling for life jackets amid the chaos as the other ship made a full starboard impact. It is hard to imagine the force of the ocean engulfing the ship. The power and strength of the ocean tossed the men against the bulkheads of the ship as if they were toys being flung by a child having a temper tantrum. I don't know if there was an explosion or a fire, but I imagine the men on the deck were flung overboard by the impact. I can picture men falling twenty, thirty feet, if not more into the dark depths of the ocean and seeing nothing but bubbles as the men hit the water. I can only imagine the impact it must have had on one's body. I wonder if the panic of some of these men made their hearts stop. Did some have heart attacks before reaching the water? Did they dissociate? Because of the speed at which they were falling, I wonder how deep they sank into the darkness of the ocean before rising to the top and getting some air.

When I heard this story, I thought about the Titanic and how terrifying that experience must have been. I was told everyone had to jump ship. My father had a friend who could not swim and was terrified of the water. My father said he tried to convince him to jump and that he would make sure he would survive in the water. His friend was so afraid that my father was unable to persuade him to jump. His friend died on the ship as the ship went down. This had a lasting effect on my dad. He made sure that his children would all be able to swim, and he taught all of us how to survive in the water. We learned how to swim at a very early age, most likely out of the guilt my father felt from not being able to save his friend.

My dad was the middle child and the peacemaker. But being the peacemaker doesn't always serve you well. My experience treating people for over twenty years has taught me that being the peacemaker results in having difficulty setting boundaries when it is necessary in order to avoid conflict as much as possible. When my dad was inconsistent with his discipline, regardless if it was with his kids or if it was being inconsistent with his wife, this waffling set the stage for conflict, which was what my father desperately wanted to avoid. This wavering behavior produced confusion for the family.

To my surprise, I suspect my dad was afraid of women. He always said, "Women rule the world," and based on his tone, I could tell he was not happy about that. He was afraid of his very strong-willed mother. My mother told me a story about my dad coming home very late one night. The only way my mother would be able to control my father was by threatening to tell his mother if he ever did that again. She told me he never stayed out late again. I feel that my mother sharing this with me was very inappropriate, as I was probably around ten years old at the time. This was the beginning of her sharing information about their marital relationship and on some level, parentifying me. This became a pattern of mixed messages for me because my mother would debase me at times and elevate my status in the family at other times.

Being very young when I heard this story, I have no recollection of my dad ever being out of the house late in the evening. I remember my dad being in a bowling league, but he always returned home before my bedtime. My dad, at times, was unable to stand up to my mother, which was unfortunate for everyone. It was unfortunate for him because he became a prisoner of my mother. My father inconsistently set limits with my mother, allowing her to behave in ways that were detrimental to all of us.

When I was divorcing the father of my children, I had a conversation with my father regarding my marriage and comparing my ex to my mother. This was a very rare discussion that was a once-in-a-lifetime conversation, which lasted about two minutes. My dad asked me if I ever felt loved by my mother. When I said no, he told me he never felt loved by her either. And that was as far as it went...the end of the conversation! I did happen to ask him, years before, what he loved about my mother and his answer was very interesting. He said, "She's a good cook." As far as I'm concerned, this is not a good reason to stay married. With that being said, my dad not feeling loved by my mother is a good example of her incapacity to engage in intimacy with anyone including her husband.

Decades later, I came to find out that he had considered divorcing her but feared she would get all his money...not that they had a substantial amount of money. I think there was more to him staying with her than just money. My mother took care of his every need; he did very little for himself. He was a victim of his culture and generation. My father would not have been happy living alone, but I do wonder how happy he really was living with my mother, as even on her best day she was impossible to live with.

My dad rarely went against my mother's decisions in front of us children, which, on one hand, is important for children. We knew our parents were a united front. This is an essential parenting skill that all children benefit from, otherwise children will split and manipulate the parents and the children will have difficulty with boundaries. However, agreeing with my mother was detrimental not only for me and my siblings but also for him. It is possible that if he had stood up to my mother, privately, more often, they might have made better parenting decisions. This would have given us a more positive sense of self and better coping skills instead of leaving us with a perception of our own incompetence.

The consequences of my dad's good nature were damaging for the entire family. My father's even-tempered attitude was overshadowed by my mother's anxiety. And because of that, he was never able to show her a different way to parent. She was never able to observe, or emulate, a different way to manage a situation when it came to parenting. He pacified my mom to avoid conflict. By not holding my mother responsible for her actions, he allowed her to oppress us. He allowed his children to become dependent on her. This created, in all three of us, such low self-esteem that we were never able to feel a sense of accomplishment. No sense of feeling good about ourselves and no sense that we could possibly do anything without being dependent on her.

Because my dad rarely stood up to my mother, it led me to believe he had no backbone. With that being the case, as children, because he rarely said anything, the old threat "Wait till your father gets home" left us actually wondering what that meant. Was the belt going to come out, or was he just going to let it slide? As children, we were scared because we were not always sure how he was going to react when we were in trouble. "Trouble" was undefined. Hence, an ever-present sense of anticipatory anxiety was always in the air.

But my dad was inconsistent in how he related not only to my mother but also how he related to me. There were many times when he would allow my mother to control everything, and then there were times when he would stand up to her, confront her absurd behavior. As for me, he was able to advise and teach me about how to budget money in ways that were so accurate and appropriate, while there were other times when he completely insulted me and deflated my self-esteem. This highlights his inconsistent behavior.

This inconsistency is a very good example of how a disorganized attachment disorder originates. Disorganized attachment is an insecure attachment style as an outcome of being abused or traumatized during childhood. People who have this disorder have a need to belong, to connect to others, while at the same time having a fear of letting them in because they feel they will eventually be rejected. As adults, these individuals may end up with romantic partners who are just as unavailable and frightening as their parents were. So, between my father and my mother, it was a losing battle. Not only did that damage me but it hurt my siblings as well.

Trish was a good-hearted person but was unable to do anything on her own. Dominic, the middle child and the peacemaker, desperately needed to be liked and surrounded himself with lots of people, whom he thought were his friends. These friends fed his fragile ego. I, on the other hand, was labeled as the rebel. I was seen as the troublemaker and, usually, went against the establishment. No one was going to control me, which, I must say, got me in trouble at times. My self-esteem was in the gutter, and I bought into the idea that I could not do anything without my mother's approval. This resulted in a constant battle between my need for independence and dependence. I often wonder whether all three of us might have been more emotionally functional if my father had had more of an input on how we were raised.

But my dad did a good job providing for us. He worked for his uncle learning a craft, custom-made kitchen cabinets. He was very talented. He could make anything. He was so talented that people like Frank Gifford and Alan Alda hired him to do work in their houses. Just about everything in our house growing up had his signature on it. He made us our first skateboards. He even built a house in Wildwood, NJ, in the early sixties, and being in Wildwood was probably the happiest time in my life living under my parents' roof.

Originally, Wildwood was a prescription given to my paternal grandmother by her doctor for her arthritis. The doctor told her the salt air would do her good. My dad's family would travel down to Wildwood prior to the Garden State Parkway having been built. It would take them eight hours to get to Wildwood from Brooklyn. I cannot imagine what that ride must have been like. No AC in the car, no place to stop and go to the bathroom, and no place to eat. But I'm sure somewhere in the car there were potato and egg, veal and peppers, and eggplant sandwiches to keep them all satisfied. The parkway opened in 1954, the year I was born, and was completed in 1956.

So, amazingly, in the early sixties my dad got his entire family together every weekend, drove the three hours on the parkway from Bergen County, and started building the duplex house. I say amazingly because my mother was completely against the idea. In her mind, it would become just another house for her to clean, even though the house was quite small. If I had to guesstimate, I would say the house was probably 750 square feet. It was an open floor plan before that was actually a thing. The living room, dining room, and kitchen were in one large space. The two bedrooms were very small. My sister and I slept in a double bed and my brother slept on a cot in the same room with barely enough room for a dresser. My parent's bedroom was not much bigger. The bathroom was off on the side of the kitchen. We were fortunate that, genetically, we were all quite thin, as two people couldn't fit in there at the same time. It was not a bathroom for someone who was claustrophobic. It was not a reading sanctuary that some people look to today. The magazine that one would read while doing their business probably would crowd the bathroom. The shower stall had barely enough room to raise your arms to shampoo your hair. And getting out of the shower and drying yourself had its own complications in and of itself. But, in a matter of a month, four weekends, the frame, roof, and windows were in. We owned one side of the duplex and my grandmother owned the other.

Wildwood meant "comfort" to me. It was less tense and the bonding between me and my siblings strengthened. We only had each other to keep us entertained. We did have a friend from Philly whose family owned a home a couple of blocks away that we all would hang with, but for the most part it was just the three of us. We had the dock that was a block away from the house and we would go and watch the boats sail by. When our cousins came down, we would go crabbing.

Crabbing was so much fun. The six of us would walk a block to the dock and put our traps in the bay. We would leave them there for hours and check on them periodically. Sometime in the afternoon we would pull up the traps and were so excited to see dozens of crabs trying to claw their way out of the cage. When we got them back to the house, my mother would bring out this huge pot and my older cousins would remove the crabs from the cage and put them into the pot. Some of the crabs would try to escape from the cages, which resulted in one of us getting nabbed by the crab claws. My mother would then have an additional pot of boiling water on the stove in preparation for dumping the crabs into the hot water. I'll never forget the squeal the crabs made hitting the boiling water. You could see the brown, olive-blue, grayish color of the crabs turn to pink as they were cooked. I can still visualize the crabs trying to escape the pot of hot water and my mother hitting the crabs with her Sicilian wooden spoon. I think that was the worst part, which was all forgotten when my mother served the spaghetti with crab sauce. So tasty! My mother was a very good cook. That's something I really miss.

Wildwood was my first introduction to comic books. There was a small convenience store several blocks away from our house. The three of us would walk there frequently to buy comic books for twenty-five cents (my favorites were *Betty and Veronica*). We called it "the mean lady store" because the owner had a face of stone that could sink a fleet of ships in a nanosecond. She never smiled and we never talked to her out of fear.

At night, maybe once a week, we would go to the boardwalk and go on the rides. Back then you could hear the waves crashing against the pier when you were on the rides. Today, Wildwood is the only beach in New Jersey that has not eroded but expanded. Expanded to the point that you need a buggy ride to take you from the boardwalk to the water.

Wildwood has always been a special place for me. Whenever I go to Cape May, I drive through Wildwood, just to look at the house my dad built. In June of 2023, my cousin was over and we took him and his wife to Cape May for the day, as they had never been there. On the way back from Cape May, I asked my cousin if he would like to see the house my dad built. So, we arrived at the house and I said to everyone, "Let's get out of the car." As I stood in the front of the house, someone came out of the house. I asked, "Are you the owner?" She said, "Yes." I then said, "My dad built this house." The owner became animated, radiant, grinning from ear to ear. She was so excited to meet the daughter of the person who had built this house. I was overwhelmed by how welcoming she was toward me. She invited all of us into the house.

Her parents purchased the house in 1964. She first took us into the house that my grandmother owned, which was the mirror image of the house my parents owned. It was a bit more up to date. Then we walked two steps to the other side of the duplex house, which we had owned. Much to my surprise, not much had been updated. The stove, kitchen cabinets, chandelier, and two chairs in the living room were the original furniture and appliances from when my parents first decorated the house. The flooring in my parents' bedroom was the original tile floor; brown, of course, because that was my dad's favorite color. Being in the house that my dad built took me back many years. It was very emotional for me, as all the memories were pleasant ones. Wildwood was always a place of tranquility and calmness for me. Tranquility and calmness were emotions that I rarely experienced in my childhood. For my mother, it was an additional stressor because all the responsibilities were on her. My dad was up north working and came down on weekends. This increased her anxiety, and for the crabs, it was always a fatal outcome.

All in all, my dad made a good living but never good enough for my mother. It was never enough for my mother; however, we were well provided for. My dad was a good man but very gender specific in his attitudes toward women. Despite the independence and power that my grandmother and great-grandmother had possessed, he still believed that women had a specific place in society, which was in the home. One would think that being raised by strong women he would have had more respect for their achievements. Unfortunately, his mindset and beliefs never changed. He was a victim of his generation, trapped within the confines of his own masculinity.

My grandmother's and great-grandmother's strengths were remarkable. Because they were midwives, they were the only ones in the neighborhood in Brooklyn who had access to a phone. I've only heard a few stories about their careers and realize I most likely get my emotional strength from them.

One evening, my great-grandmother received a call in the middle of the night to deliver a baby. She asked her brother, my Uncle Corky, to drive her to the home. I have this image of what this car might have looked like. Thank God for running boards back then, as they both would have needed a hoist to get into the car, due to their small stature. I can picture my Uncle Corky, who was no bigger than my great-grandmother, sitting in the car with this very large steering wheel resembling the helm of a cruise ship. I can see his arms stretched out as far as his arms could possibly stretch to grab the wheel to maintain control of the car. My great-grandmother always sat in the back of the car. She appeared to be mesmerized by the rain beating down on the windshield, watching the wipers wash the rain away, as the two wipers went in the opposite direction of each other, with a metal piece in the windshield dividing the driver's side and the passenger's side. She could hear the raindrops hitting the car and hoped she would arrive to her destination on time.

On that rainy night in Brooklyn, her brother turned down the wrong street. The wrong street meant the Mafia was going to "take care" of someone. Her brother was forced to stop the car as a man stood in front of the car prohibiting him from going any further. He rolled down his window and felt something cold pressing against his head. It was not the cold air or the rain hitting his head, he felt a small circular black metal object placed against his temple. I can only imagine the disbelief, fear, and lack of control he experienced at that moment. I wonder if he was able to comprehend the reality of the situation, almost feeling and hearing the gunpowder explode as the bullet penetrates his brain. I wonder if, in that split second, he saw his body rise above himself and visualized the splattered blood against the window as his body draped, lifeless, over the front seat of the car. Or, I wonder if this petite man from Naples never felt any of the above emotions and thought about his sister's safety, while thinking: "I can take this guy. Could this be a dream, am I imagining this, or is this my reality at this moment?"

My great-grandmother, who was barely five foot and very petite, poked her head from the back seat to the front seat, touching the upholstery of the front seat with her right hand, and recognized who was holding the gun. The way the story was told to me, I concluded my great-grandmother was calm, assertive, strong, and confident. She asked "Harry" what he was doing. Harry, shocked and stunned that he was addressed by name, said, "Rose, is that you?" She said, "Yes, Harry, what are you doing?" Harry did not answer but let them be on their way. My grandmother and great-grandmother delivered many babies for the Mafia and were respected within the community. I guess one can say they were protected.

There was another time when my great-grandmother went to deliver a baby for the Mafia. "He," whoever he was, was in the kitchen, and was having difficulty breaking the neck of a chicken for dinner. My great-grandmother noticed that "he" looked distraught, anxious, not knowing what to do, while holding the chicken by its neck and watching the chicken squirm. "He" was also squirming (probably more nervous than the chicken). My great-grandmother, again barely five feet, asked him what the problem was, as she tuned into his nonverbal behavior. Not being able to admit "he" was unable to kill the chicken, he stood there with a blank stare on his face. And here's where I believe I get my bluntness from. Shoot from the hip. Say what you mean and mean what you say. She looked at him with no fear at all and said, "You kill people for a living, you can't kill a chicken?" Without giving it a second thought, she grabbed the chicken away from him and "crack," broke the chicken's neck. Back then, killing the chicken was more about survival for my great-grandmother. If you were unable to kill the chicken, you weren't going to eat. The Mafia did not have the poverty issue that most people had back then. My grandmother and great-grandmother's strength came from hardship and most likely, genetics. So, for me and my siblings, when my mother would say "If you don't stop doing that, I will break your neck," we sort of took it seriously.

And then there were the stories that my dad said were "inferred." Stories that were never spoken about. Those were the babies that didn't make it. When a hermaphrodite (intersex) or extremely disabled baby was delivered, my grandmother/great-grandmother would make a decision to not allow the mother and baby to suffer a terrible life.

And that was my dad's family. The majority of the time you knew where you stood. There was little guesswork, some apprehension, but definitely no manipulation. The main difference between my mom and dad was the absence of tension and anxiety with my dad. My dad was even-tempered and a somewhat reasonable man, who was at times unpredictable. But I wasn't close to him either. I was not "daddy's little girl," or at least I did not feel like I was. There were no overt signs of affection from either of my parents. There was an absence of intimacy coming at me from both directions.

Chapter 5

THE SICILIAN MOTHER

I can spot a Sicilian from ten feet away. This capacity probably has no socially redeeming value, but it comes in handy. There is a certain air and attitude about them that any Sicilian can pick up on immediately. The Sicilian mother is a challenge. She is opinionated, loud, impatient, controlling, critical, and can always predict the future; she has paranormal powers. She is a "doctor" who diagnoses everyone, except she does not have a medical degree. In my family, the only degree she had was one of arrogance. The Sicilian mother will always publicly defend her children, no matter how wrong her children are…until she gets them home. Most Sicilian mothers are openly affectionate toward their children when they are surrounded by others; most likely to show what wonderful mothers they are. However, after the public display of support, when she gets you home and into her domain, she gives you "the look," and then the wooden spoon comes out and she waves it in the air saying, "How could you do that to me!"

But these characteristics are not exclusive to just Sicilian women. Sicilian men can be just as difficult and impatient as the women. In 2014, my husband and I traveled to Italy and spent a week in Sicily. I wanted to get in touch with my roots and taste the foods that I grew up with from the "mother country." The strangest feeling came over me when we landed in Sicily. I felt oddly comfortable. I say oddly because the Italian culture, for the greater part of my life, gave me a great deal of angst. But I felt like I was home. We landed in Palermo where my maternal grandparents were born, and we were waiting for our luggage to come out. The construction of the luggage carousel chute was a bit strange. It was several feet high and had lots of curves that prevented the luggage from flowing smoothly onto the carousel. Pretty much a metaphor for the Sicilian personality. The luggage got jammed at the top of the carousel chute. The Sicilians started yelling and became very angry. I thought to myself, yes, I am home! I noticed my husband became a bit anxious. Knowing "my people," I told my husband "Just keep watching and wait for the show to begin," as I knew "my people" were *not* going to wait very long for someone to unjam the luggage. It is my experience that Sicilians have no patience and impulsively take matters into their own hands. So, seconds later, this Sicilian man had all he could take. While he continued to yell, he had obviously seen something that had attracted his attention, his own suitcase! He literally climbed several feet up the carousel chute to where the luggage was jammed, got his luggage, climbed down and the rest of the luggage flowed with him down the chute. I turned to my husband and said, "See, what did I tell you?" Oddly enough, our luggage was directly behind this man's luggage.

The most obvious trait of a Sicilian mother, and probably of most Italian mothers, is the food issue. You will never go hungry, and you will never have enough food on your plate or in your stomach. Regardless of your weight, the Sicilian mother will always tell you "You look too skinny." Then the questions come: "Are you eating properly? What are you eating? When are you eating and how much? You should be having pasta at least once a day. What do you mean you're on a diet?" And then there are the times when she recognizes you have put on weight. She criticizes you for looking fat and tells you "You will never find a man if you don't watch your weight." Simultaneously as she is talking, she continues to pile the food onto your plate, repeating to you how men do not like heavy women. I wonder if eating disorders originated in Sicily, and I wonder if Sicilians coined the phrase "mixed messages."

Sicilians can't accept no for an answer. This is what mealtimes looked like. First of all, there is always pasta along with a meat or fish dish. The Sicilian mother will always serve you so you have no say in how much food you will eat. She will pile the food onto your plate as if it is your last meal on death row. You must finish everything, and if you don't, she will assume, since you did not eat fast enough, that the food got cold. She will then put more hot food onto your plate. If you finish everything on your plate, she will ask you if you want more. This is not a question for you to answer. This is a rhetorical question. A question that does not require a response. The Sicilian mother does not give you time to think about or process the question before another pile of ziti is on your plate with at least two to three meatballs. And *you must* finish in order to get dessert…and you cannot refuse dessert. Not eating food cooked by an Italian is an insult to the cook, and the Sicilian mother sees it as a cardinal sin.

Coffee is served after almost every meal. I was too young to remember when I started drinking coffee because I don't ever remember *not* drinking coffee. I know I had a cup before I went to school, so I have to assume I was around four years old. It is insane to think they gave us coffee when we were so young; however, it was a cultural thing. I did not repeat that tradition with my own kids, however. I have now been drinking coffee for sixty-four years.

Sicilian mothers have ESP and eyes in the back of their heads. They always know what's going to happen before it happens. They would have "the feeling." Remember my grandmother had the "feeling" that something bad would happen just before my grandfather died. My mother's biggest thing was to wear a hat and bring an umbrella before you leave the house. "Ma, it's sixty degrees out, I don't need a hat," and she would say, "It's going to get cold." Bear in mind this was before Google. And guess what, somehow, she knew the temperature would drop twenty degrees or it would rain, despite the bright sunshine when we left the house. She always seemed to be right. She always had to be right and could never admit when she was wrong. The narcissism, and Sicilians can be very narcissistic.

In addition, Sicilian mothers are also the fashion police. One can spend hours picking out an outfit for an event only to hear: "You're wearing *that*, with all the clothes you have in your closet, and you have a lot. You have to clean out your closet, it's too cluttered, no wonder you cannot find anything nice to wear. It's this house that you bought with small closets. I never liked this house. Maybe you need to expand your closet so you can find your nice clothes, so when company comes over, they won't think you are such a slob and blame me for being a bad mother. I don't want people to think I raised a pig. All you need to do is push this wall out a few feet, because when things are neater, you will be able to see the dirt more and keep a cleaner house. You know you can do a better job of keeping your house clean. I shouldn't have to come here and clean up after you all the time." Like I ever wanted my mother to come and clean my house. What you wear is another reflection of the mother. What you clean and *don't* clean to her satisfaction is a reflection of the mother. And the best line of all is when Italians say, "You never know when the Pope will stop by."

But it does not stop there. Before there were home security cameras like Ring, Arlo, or Cove, there was the Sicilian mother who was the original security system. The Sicilian mother knew everything that went on in the neighborhood. The Sicilian mother with her flowery apron on, her hair pulled back into a bun, and the impeccable hearing that only certain animals could also be sensitive to. The Sicilian mother would slither toward the venetian blinds on the window, and using her index finger and thumb she would carefully separate the two vanes of the blinds. While she believed she was quiet enough to sneak a peak of the outside world, one could always hear the aluminum blinds, pinging, rasping, and the sharp clinking of the blinds.

Unfortunately, this was a learned behavior I wish I never adopted. Whenever I am on the beach, a place that is relaxing and calming, and after I set up my beach chair and organize my beach bag, flip-flops, and cooler, relaxation doesn't actually appear. My husband sits in his chair, opens his book, and is good to go. For me, it is very different. I am looking around, assessing my surroundings. Unable to sit and soak up the sun, I am concerned about who is doing what. As I am appraising the situation, I notice who is breaking the rules by having these large tents that are prohibited on our beach. I hear others with their radios playing rap music too loud, which I despise, and those who decide to spray themselves with sunscreen on a windy day that inevitably blows our way. I only start to physically cringe when I witness a parent abandoning their small toddler left sleeping on their beach blanket as they go into the ocean to cool off. The child awakens screaming for their missing parents. It is impossible for me to focus on anything but that child, alone on the blanket, scared, confused, and feeling abandoned. I am consumed with thoughts of someone grabbing that child and walking away with them, while the parents are oblivious and focusing on their own pleasures. My mind is racing, my eyes glued on this child as I already have a plan in my head as to how I will save this child if such a thing happens. I wonder what kind of trust issues this kid will have throughout life. Eventually, the parent returns to the blanket to comfort her child who has been crying for what seemed to be about fifteen minutes. I then spend the rest of the time wondering if we should move further away from the crowd. By the time I settle in, it's time for dinner, we pack up our stuff and go back to our unit. This unconscious process, which I internalized from my mother playing neighborhood watch, makes it difficult to individuate from her. My husband continues to calmly sit in his chair, reading his book, and proceeds to turn to the very next page, oblivious to what is happening around him.

As you can see, it is almost impossible to get out from underneath the Sicilian mother's vise grip and the hold she has on you. They want all their children to live very close to them. Sicilian mothers are like packing material, Styrofoam peanuts, deceptively light and fluffy. However, once you gravitate toward the illusion of fluffiness, you can never rid yourself of it. Their static electricity clings to you forever. These Styrofoam peanuts appear to multiply on your body, spreading like a virus. Once you brush them off your arm, you find them on your shoulder. You brush them off your shoulder, they're now in your hair. You try to pull them out of your hair only to have them stick to your fingers. It gives you the appearance of protection; however, they bury you almost to the point of suffocation.

After I got married the first time, I moved twenty minutes away from my mother, and I thought my mother was going to have a stroke. I could actually see the blood vessels in her brain burst, as her speech became impaired, becoming paralyzed on one side of her body, grabbing to hold on to the furniture before possibly falling to the floor. While in my head, I could feel the dopamine levels increase, as I just giddily watched her as she unraveled. Twenty minutes meant gas the car up, rotate the tires, clean the windshield, and check the fluids. It also meant losing more control of me and not having me visit her as often. To a Sicilian mother, having her children visit often is on the same level as eating the food she cooks. There is no logical order of "what's important" to her. Everything is important and a top priority: eating her food, calling her daily, visiting her frequently, and being just like her.

And then there were the required habitual daily/weekly phone calls. And the phone only works one way, as Sicilian mothers only know how to answer the phone, not dial and call someone. When I was younger, I called my mother almost daily. As I matured and became more independent, I would call her weekly. But when I really started to extract myself from her, I would call her when I wanted to call her. The conversations would go like this. Ring, ring, ring. My mother would say, "Hello," and I would say, "Hi, ma." She would say, "Who is this?" As I exhaled, feeling my esophagus burning as the flames cascaded out of my mouth and as my eyes rolled back into my head, I would say, "It's your daughter." She would say, "Oh hi, Trish." I would then say, "No ma, try again." After a few seconds of silence, I would say, "It's me, Diane." She would say, "*Who?*" and I would repeat my name. "Oh Diane, I thought you were dead, but since I couldn't find your obituary in the newspaper, I thought maybe you had an accident and the police were too busy to come and tell me. I didn't know what happened to you since it's been so long since you called"—as I thought to myself, it's only been a week—"I thought you forgot you had a mother." If only! After we would get beyond that, she would say, "So, what's new?" and, literally, two minutes into the conversation, she would say, "Not to change the subject but," and go on about my aunts or how my cousins would call their mothers daily or who is fighting with whom. After dealing with this for a while, I decided to try a new tactic. Ring, ring, ring, "Hi, ma." She would say, "Who is this?" and I would say, "Oh, I must have the wrong number, sorry," and hang up. She stopped playing that game after that.

And then there were the weapons! The men carried guns, but the women wielded wooden spoons. There were two things that kept children, as well as crabs, of Sicilian mothers in line. The look and the wooden spoon. A child would never step out of line when their mother had the wooden spoon in her hand and was making gravy. If you got hit with the wooden spoon while she was making gravy, you would wonder whether it was gravy or blood that was dripping down on your body. A child never brought a problem to their mother when she was cooking, especially if you did not know how she was going to react. The look was searing, with eyes that were so piercing you would think your head would split open. The look when the eyebrows came together in the middle of her forehead. Her forehead wrinkled with a look of contempt on her face, the scowl. Both the look and the spoon could stop you dead in your tracks!

The trials and tribulations of having a Sicilian mother served as a learning experience. The grip she had on me was tighter than the rusty Vise-Grips my dad had in the basement, and it took decades and tens of thousands of dollars toward therapy as well as WD-40 to loosen those pliers she had around my neck. When I was in my fifties, one of my therapists said to me after I had bitterly complained about my mother that my mother was old and that she needed me more than I needed her. My therapist said my mother no longer had any power over me. The only power she had over me was the power I gave her. Those words were extremely helpful to me.

I am sure these behaviors and traits are not exclusive to just Sicilians. This was my experience and how my Sicilian mother behaved. I know there are many other cultures in which mothers exhibit these similar behaviors. With that being said, many of my Sicilian clients have described and experienced their mothers/parents in the same way.

Being able to objectively look at my culture and my family of origin, I consciously tried not to repeat some of these negative traditions with my own kids. I didn't want to traumatize my kids the way I was traumatized, so I keep my wooden spoon in the drawer and out of sight. I never threatened them with the wooden spoon. The "look," however…

Chapter 6

THE POWER OF THE UNCONSCIOUS

A Perfect Match—My parents met in Brooklyn, NY

My mother was from East New York and my dad was from Crown Heights. The benefit to my mother having several sisters close in age meant they were never at a loss for men. All of the sisters were quite sociable and easily attracted male attention. I can only imagine the revolving door of guys walking through the house. And yes, these male prospects, young bachelors, were all Italian, at least for the first go around. Two of my aunts divorced, and one of them got remarried to a Jewish man. I have no idea if that was an issue for my grandmother, because in the 1960s, divorce was taboo. However, my aunt had two young boys to raise, and raising them all on her own back then would have been more than difficult. She had to expand her options to more than just Sicilians.

Initially, my dad dated one of my aunts a couple of times. Evidently, there were no sparks between them; they were more like friends. My dad asked my aunt if she would mind if he asked her sister out on a date. Although my dad had access to a phone, my mother did not. Snail mail was the only source of communication, and that's when one could actually depend on the mail being delivered in a reasonably timely fashion. So, he wrote my mom a letter explaining his interest in her.

I do not have any of the letters my mom sent to my dad, however; she did keep one letter she received from my dad. Maybe my dad saved her letters, and after they were married, she might have thrown them out. My mother saved very little and threw out what she considered junk. My mother was also extremely vain and private, so it is possible she did not want anyone to see her letters in which she could have possibly expressed any kind of positive emotions or emotions in general. One theory why my mother saved my dad's letter is because he described her in a very positive light, which clearly fed into her narcissism.

May 29, 1947
Dear Lee,

This letter will no doubt take you by surprise—you may have even forgotten who I am, having seen me only twice. You only know me as Pat, your sister Annie's friend and you'll probably be wondering why I'm writing to you and not to her. However, I've been thinking about this for some time and this is one impulse I can't curb.

You see Lee, Annie and I went out a few times and I must say we had a lot of fun kidding each other along. But we weren't really interested in each other because basically we see things differently. We could have gone out together indefinitely without ever becoming more than the best of friends. You are probably wondering what you have to do with all this.

The fact is, Lee, that I've been thinking about you since the first time I met you and more so since the second time. What can a fellow do who finds himself in such a predicament, nothing. I guess except try to tell you about it. You see a guy always has a good idea of the kind of a girl he's looking for— and to me you seemed to be it. How can anyone tell on such a short acquaintance??…well, it's quite possible—you may know what I mean.

In the first place, you were very friendly and sociable and you made me feel right at home. However, you did that without knocking yourself out, but just by being natural—it showed breeding and poise, qualities that are rare in my neck of the woods. That may not be much in itself, but you also are warm, friendly, and you have a sense of humor. I don't know if you recall the remark that "bad weather brings bad company," but you said that knowing, of course, that I would take that in the spirit of jest and wouldn't be offended. What I am getting at is that we understand one another and under more favorable conditions, who can tell what might have turned out.

I don't know how you will receive this letter, Lee. You may be quite shocked by the whole thing, or then you may find it amusing…possibly, you are undecided how you feel. Anyway, that's what I'm hoping—that you are undecided. In the event, let's give each other a chance to become better acquainted. I don't know how I can run across you, but I'm hoping that you will, at least, acknowledge this letter (it's more like a confession) by dropping me a line or two in return. I would like to correspond with you—you can write about anything you like—people, hobbies, books, music or better still yourself. I'll close now hoping to hear from you.

Sincerely,
Pat

If this was a movie, I would cast Jimmy Stewart and Bette Davis to play my parents in this black-and-white cinema. I can picture and feel my dad's softness, the calmness that he had the ability to project, as he's writing this letter, flattering her. I could actually feel how much he yearns for her and wants to make a good impression. I can envision him looking for a quiet place to write in a house full of people. I visualize him, situated at a table with pen in hand, contemplating his every word before putting it on paper, while sitting in a pile of crumpled scripts, first drafts, lying on the floor, which leaned against the leg of the chair. The twinkle in his eyes, hoping she would respond positively to his letter. Like the characters that Jimmy Stewart portrayed in his films, he was meticulous, approachable, courteous, and helpful.

While on the other hand, as the music changes, the scene shifts, and I can only imagine the thoughts my mother had when she received this letter. I can see an expression of confusion and inquisitiveness on her face, thinking this letter was meant for her sister, when this piece of mail was delivered. Once she opens the envelope, I have this vision of these Bette Davis eyes, focused, intent, absorbed, and consuming the words. As she reads them, they are feeding into her need to be praised, feeding into her ego. As a spectator in the theater viewing this movie, I am a bit baffled as to how this romantic fantasy will end. Time for popcorn.

Now back to reality. There is so much to unpack here. I wish my dad could have introduced me to "Lee." That "Lee" might have been a better mother to me. I never saw the side of her that was described in the letter, and I don't know how long it took for those traits that my father was so attracted to to wane. But the unconscious is very powerful and always at work!

I am not shocked that my father was attracted to her, coming from a family of very strong women and seeing my mother as poised (her perfectionistic quality) and of good breeding. I never knew my mother to be sarcastic or have a sense of humor. The comment my mother made that my dad mentions in the letter about "bad weather brings bad company" could have been a projection on my mother's part. My father had no idea how much of a storm was actually coming down the road. Mother Nature, at times, can just sneak up on you, like a tornado, a tsunami, a flash flood, an earthquake, or an avalanche; there is not always

Diane Harth

adequate warning. But my dad was a patient man, and he tolerated a great deal from her.

As humans, we are attracted to others on an unconscious level, possibly to fill a void within ourselves. In many cases we are attracted to and gravitate toward a person who is similar to the parent we have the most issues with. We do this in the hope of changing our partner, which in our unconscious mind can change the difficult parent. This never works. This either ends in divorce or makes for a very unhealthy, unhappy life.

My parent's marriage laid the foundation for the dysfunctional marriage that I entered into with the father of my children. Being exposed to their continued dysfunction, I learned this is the way marriage is. When I fell in love with Oscar, unconsciously, it was a requirement for me to repeat the mistakes my parents made, because that seemed correct, as incorrect as it was. This is a good explanation of how I came to marry the father of my children.

But my parent's marriage was "a match made in heaven." My mother was controlling and my dad was the peacemaker. My mom would yell and my dad would eventually cave in. Not a good example to show kids how to resolve conflict. But my mom would have never married someone who was controlling; she needed someone who would tolerate her neurosis. My dad married someone, on some level, who was like his mother…strong. But my mother was strong only in the sense that she had little tolerance for anything. The game they played was very confusing. They controlled each other, taking turns being submissive, giving the message that one must be either controlling or submissive; never equal. This is not the atmosphere for a healthy marriage. Hence, the reason why all their children wound up divorced.

My brother gave me this letter several years ago after my parents had both passed on, and it was the first time I had ever read it. The letter triggered several emotions. The first emotion I felt was how genuine, sweet, and romantic my dad was. Something I never saw in him. He was completely enthralled with my mom. He was soft and caring. I was shocked at the respect he showed her in the letter, not that he ever disrespected her. What jarred me was I never saw this softness in him as a parent. My father's parenting style was based on the premise that children must respect parents. But his idea of respect was to put fear into his children so they would listen. I will assume his Catholic education had something to do with this particular thought process. But this is not teaching respect; this is teaching fear. This is instructing children how to be silent and how not to express themselves. This is oppression. This is probably why I felt like I was always in trouble. I couldn't keep my mouth shut. At an early age, I unconsciously felt controlled by everyone around me: my parents, teachers, society. This can explain why I did so poorly in school. I was unable to be emotionally disciplined enough to be part of a group. In school, the "group" was the classroom. This is probably one reason why I never participated in any extracurricular activities at school.

My father obviously saw something in my mother that was never seen by her children. My mother lost herself, her identity, when she got married. When I became an adult and was able to objectively observe my parents' relationship, I saw my father as a prisoner of my mother's strong hold on him. He avoided any kind of conflict with her until he couldn't anymore and felt forced to stand up to her. He never challenged her about how she disciplined us…or at least not with me. I did observe Dominic getting in trouble with them; however, the rules were always more intense with respect to me. For me, a minor infraction resulted in a severe punishment. For Dominic, a major violation resulted in a slap on the wrist.

My parents both projected these prisoner-like feelings that they experienced onto each other. My dad's prison sentence, as carried out by my mother, entailed his being manipulated into his giving in to her in his peacemaker role. My father, as the warden, only allowed my mother to work outside of the home at Christmastime when expenses exceeded what they could afford. My mother was unable to reach her full potential outside of the family home because of cultural and gender stereotypes. She was insecure about her own identity and about being a woman. She was prohibited from spreading her wings and exploring the outside world by working outside of the home. She was only able to explore the outside world from within the four walls of the house. She became the warden within the family, having complete control over everyone. This was particularly true with respect to me. I was a representation of my mother's loss of the personal control over her life. My mother, on some level, felt forced to have a third child. She felt like she had no control of herself and limited control over my father; therefore, this third child had to be dominated. It was the only thing she *could* control, aside from keeping the house clean.

My mother was always ashamed about dropping out of school and being uneducated. She had the desire to grow and expand her knowledge, but that too was prohibited by my father. Any outside curricular activity was frowned upon by my dad. Working outside the home or becoming educated would have enabled her to socialize with her peers and possibly be open to others' points of views, expanding her own ideas of the world. He said, "If you work outside the home, you will only become more upset and anxious about the house not being as clean as you would like it." However, I don't believe my dad would have wanted to pick up the slack in the house, caring for the kids, and possibly helping with dinner.

I was a reminder of what my mother was unable to control. I was a reminder of what she could have been and what she was not. A reminder of her strong will and what she no longer was. A reminder of her own rebellion by marrying a Neapolitan. Her rebellion could only be seen in her controlling behavior. I was the trigger for her reexperiencing her trauma and I paid the price.

Chapter 7

THE NOT GOOD
ENOUGH MOTHER

My parents got married in 1948, and Trish was born in 1950. They lived in Brooklyn for a short time before moving to Lodi, New Jersey. They moved to New Jersey because my father worked there and moving made his commute to work easier. Both my sister and brother were born in Lodi.

My sister was the second grandchild born on both sides of the family and my mother had lots of time for her. I heard stories of how my mother read to my sister every day or at least until Dominic was born three years later. I believe there was a pregnancy prior to my mother becoming pregnant with Dominic that ended in a miscarriage.

Based on what my mother told me, Dominic was a handful when he was an infant. Considering how often I heard this, I can conclude that it was not just me she was unable to tolerate. She had no coping skills for anything that was less than perfect or anything that was difficult. Dominic cried every moment of the day until my father came home. I am sure that drove my mother a bit crazy, as it would any mother, not being able to comfort her son and having a toddler running around at the same time. I am sure she was exhausted. But he was the Italian son, which came with certain privileges.

My brother was born in October of 1953 and in the spring of 1954 my mother found herself pregnant, again, with me. But this wasn't a surprise or a mistake. I was labeled an accident. An accident is defined in the dictionary as "an unfortunate incident that happens unexpectedly and unintentionally, typically resulting in damage or injury." A mistake is defined as "an act or judgment that is misguided or wrong." Mistakes can be corrected, can be worked out and sometimes work out for the best. I was labeled an "accident." I was unwanted, as I have been told many times since I was a child. An accident cannot be corrected. This accident had consequences for both me and my mother. My mother was unable to accept me and projected all those unwanted feelings and emotions that she was unable to cope with onto me.

During my decades of being in treatment and discussing my mother, I have had a few therapists tell me they suspect my mother was possibly assaulted at some point in her life. I have no way of knowing if that is true. However, when more than one therapist tells you this, I assume there must be something to it.

This hypothesis is not too far off from things my mother had actually described to me. When I was a teen, my mother would occasionally tell me about her sex life with my father. I can still picture myself standing by the stairs in the living room with my mother as she told me this story. I have no recollection of how this subject came about, most likely because I blocked it out, but she would say to me, "Your father always wants to have sex with me and I really don't want to." She also told me that he would, occasionally, force himself on her. I wouldn't dare to be inquisitive and ask her about any details. That was taboo for a child to ask, but in the same context, how inappropriate was this conversation? No child should be told about their parents' sex life. What was astounding about this is she *never* educated me about what exactly "sex" was, let alone the nature of any type of relationships, intimate or otherwise. My mother never discussed her courtship with my dad. This led to a very confusing message. What was she trying to convey to me? Was the message that my father was still attracted to her or that men only want sex from women? On one hand, she parentified me, and on the other hand, she infantilized me by controlling me and keeping me ignorant. This ambivalence was a manifestation of her own anxiety. My hypothesis for the reason she told me this story was that it was to explain her disdain for me. I am the product of her, perhaps, being forced to have sex with my father, which resulted in me being born. I am a constant reminder of her being possibly assaulted, which triggers her resentment of me. This disdain she projected onto me resulted in my low self-esteem, which has lasted a lifetime.

The message my mother sent me was sex was bad, men are bad, I was the product of this bad sex, inferring that I was bad. I believe my mother was forced to have sex with my dad, which resulted in another child. That child being me. I assume that my mother did not hold my dad responsible for the pregnancy. She projected her anger and all her unhappiness onto me. Remember it was only a few months after Dominic was born that she had to plan for another baby. She had barely recovered from the last postpartum, with a crying baby and a toddler, when she discovered there was a third child on the way. There is no way of knowing what really happened the night I was conceived, but if my father did force her to have sex with him, my therapists' hypothesis was right on the money with respect to my mother having been sexually assaulted.

I believe that to my mother, I represented the foulest, most unpleasant effect of my father's sexual need and it saddled me with the guilt and responsibility of his assault. All the taboos about sex that needed to be kept secret, to protect her sense of shame, had to be projected onto me. I am a reminder of that abuse, so my mother had to warn me and punish me simultaneously; it was her ambivalence to both protect me and punish me. She felt victimized and needed to victimize me. She victimized me in a way that assaulted me emotionally and traumatized me with respect to future sexual experiences in my life.

When my mother became pregnant with me, they were forced to move because the house in Lodi was too small for a family of five. They sold the house and moved to East Paterson, which is now Elmwood Park. My father put down a fifty-dollar deposit along with a handshake to hold the house before papers could be drawn up. The house cost $10,500. They moved in June 1954, several months before I was born. It was a comfortable house, but an unusual split-level house, with three floors. When you entered the house, you would come into the living room, which was a decent size. A coat closet was to the right and a staircase, also to the right, took you upstairs to the bedrooms. The kitchen was on the first floor just beyond the stairs. There was a small wall that the living room and kitchen shared. On that wall, on the kitchen side, were the kitchen cabinets. There was a wide opening between the living room and the dining room and an opening between the kitchen and dining room. As young kids we would run around in circles from the living room through the kitchen and dining room and back into the living room. This bothered my father so much that when the kitchen was remodeled, he built a barrier wall between the dining room and the living room, waist high and partly open; we could see into the living room from the dining room and from the dining room into the living room. He also removed the wall in the kitchen where the cabinets were hung, reconfigured it, and made it one big open space. However, by putting a divider between the living room and dining room, he took all our fun away.

The living room did not have plastic covers on the furniture, but it was always pristine. One can visualize the invisible rope surrounding the living room, like we all have seen at certain venues to prevent people from entering a prohibited area. For my mother, this invisible barrier was to keep the living room clean. This was the "no-fly" zone. Off the kitchen was a door to the garage where the washer and dryer were kept and another lower level of the basement that my dad finished off later on when we were older. I was always terrified to go into the basement and I assume it was from my night terrors. The basement really wasn't a dingy old basement. As a matter of fact, my mother kept it just as clean as the living room. She would actually wash the garage floor where my dad would park his car. Yes, this is bizarre!

There were two bedrooms and a bathroom on the second floor, and the third floor was where my parents' bedroom was located. The furniture in my brother's room and the room I shared with my sister was custom-made by my father. Dominic had wall-to-wall furniture. He had a desk with lots of shelves and cabinets for storage and a closet that he did not have to share. In the room that I was in with my sister, my dad had built two desks, dressers for us, and a nightstand. We shared a closet that was small by today's standards. She had half and I had half, but I always wound up with less than half, as she was not always considerate of someone else's space.

We all shared one bathroom. One bathroom for five people, four of whom needed to shower in the morning before leaving the house for school or work. My sister *always* monopolized the bathroom by literally being in there for hours at a time. It took years before my mother convinced my dad to build a bathroom in their bedroom, which he did. My dad was able to build a small bathroom, toilet, and sink by pushing out a small part of the house, being able to connect the plumbing easily because it was above the kitchen sink. Having a second bathroom did not alleviate the backup for the shower, but the family had an additional place to at least pee and poop.

The day my mother went into labor with me, my father's mother was at the house. I know I was born at six o'clock, but I don't know if it was morning or night. My mother always told me she did not want to go to the hospital. She always told me she did not want to have me. My grandmother told her if she didn't go to the hospital immediately, she would have a home birth. So, she went. Back then the father was not allowed in the delivery room while his wife was giving birth. So, as he had done when my siblings were born, he dropped her off at the front door of Passaic General Hospital and left. I think it was more like him slowing the car down and pushing her out.

I was described as a very easy baby. I guess I had to be. I had to unconsciously take on a different role from what my siblings displayed. My mother said I was like a loaf of bread. I stayed wherever she put me. I do not know if it was my paternal grandmother or great-grandmother who told my mother, "Keep an eye on her, she's beautiful and someone may steal her." Well, we know how that worked out.

I have to assume my sister was not very receptive to having another sibling. My brother was about fourteen months old when I was born and too young to understand that he was having a baby sister. When Dominic was born, Trish did not accept him at all. She would tell everyone she did not have a brother. That went on for a while until one day my father came home and said, "How is your baby brother doing?" She responded, "I don't have a baby brother." My father yelled at her (his voice was scary when he was mad, which wasn't that often) telling her he didn't want her to ever say that again. I am not sure if my dad spanked her at that time, but that was the last time she said that. I have no idea what her reaction was to me coming along. However, it could explain why we were never close.

Given my father's reaction to my sister dismissing having a brother, I assume my parents did not provide any comfort to my sister when I was born. I highly doubt they explained to this three-year-old that she was still loved. She had no understanding as to why Mommy and Daddy did this to her. Why did they bring home another baby when she was unable to accept the second baby? I can only imagine what it was like for my sister; fourteen months after my brother was born, I was born.

My mother did not want me, did not want to go to the hospital, and I was not given a middle name like they did for my siblings. It is no wonder this had generated a sense of isolation on my part. I grew up with a series of taboos with disproportionate punishments for only me. What some parents do not realize is that what they say to their children has consequences. These words may not intentionally be directed to hurt the child, but words do have an impact regardless of whether it is a positive or negative consequence. What I find so fascinating, as I write this, is the realization of the negativity my mother projected onto her children. We only heard the negative stories—Dominic was inconsolable and I was unwanted. I heard nothing about my sister. We never heard positive stories.

Chapter 8

THE IMPORTANCE OF TOUCH

When my mother was in the hospital, at the time when both my parents were in assisted living, she needed a pacemaker. Dominic and I (my sister had passed on by then) were at the hospital, and the doctor was discussing possible options for my mom (ironically, I was the primary health care proxy for both my parents). After the doctor explained everything, he strongly suggested a pacemaker. As I glanced over to see if Dominic was OK with my mother getting a pacemaker, I noticed a strange expression on his face. He looked a bit confused, as if he was unable to understand what the doctor was saying. He looked as if he was filled with uncertainty. He looked perplexed. I wondered if maybe, by some chance, he was reading a medical journal in the waiting room and had a medical insight about my mother's procedure. After a few seconds had passed, Dominic looked up at the doctor, looked him straight in the eyes, and without blinking, as serious as anyone can be at that moment, asked the doctor: "My mother has a heart? We never knew that." I thought for a moment the doctor would go into cardiac arrest after that comment.

There was a time when I was a young child, remembering the warmth of my mother's touch. As a young child, I suffered with terrible, chronic earaches. Probably due to genetics. My mom had small ear canals as do I, and unfortunately, I generously passed it down to my son. I remember when I was about five years old, the pain in my ears was so bad that my mother carried me around the house in the middle of the night for hours as I cried in pain. As I recall this time in my life, I can actually feel the warmth of her arms around me, cradling me, as she walked around the house. I can see the concern in her eyes of not knowing how to comfort me and not knowing how to ease my pain. This is such a vivid memory, probably because I have no other memory of my mother's touch, aside from being slapped in the face once or twice or having my hair pulled (probably why I always like short hair). This was the only time I felt safe and cared for by her. This was the only time I was able to feel the warmth from her body penetrating into my body. It was calming. I felt her presence.

My mother never hugged anyone in a way in which you can actually feel her arms wrap around you. It was more like an air hug in which her arms go around you but do not touch your body. You know like how the movie stars give air kisses. And that hug was not when we were little but as we got older. I have no recollection of being hugged as a child except for this one very specific time. It is so sad for me to recall this event, as I remember it so vividly. She obviously had this softness, the warmth, and emotional love to give at that moment. Unfortunately, most of the time she kept it hidden. My mother did not have a wall around her; it was more like she confined herself to a vault that no one, including herself, had the combination to. A vault door made of steel weighing three thousand to five thousand pounds and a foot thick; a stick of dynamite would not be able to penetrate it. This vault was a frozen chamber so cold that no warmth could ever escape it. As a result, her warmth was permanently locked in the vault. This vault contained every emotion she ever had. It was a storage chamber of unresolved issues and anxieties.

At the age of five, the earaches became so intense that it was recommended I have my tonsils and adenoids surgically removed as opposed to my mother ripping them out herself. My first surgery. I remember being excited about going into the hospital. Very odd, I must say. I remember almost running up the stairs to the entrance of the hospital, and, as a five-year-old, it seemed like there were a lot of stairs, as if it was the Spanish Steps in Rome. My excitement was most likely unconscious, knowing I had to escape this unhealthy home environment.

In retrospect and having some understanding of the unconscious, I can assume that being in the hospital meant I would be cared for and would have undivided attention, which I did not receive at home. The hospital was a place where I would not be criticized or yelled at; a place where I would not have to compete with my siblings. I must say, with all my past surgeries, and I have had many, going to the hospital was something I always looked forward to. It was a respite for me. I always knew it was a place where I would be cared for unconditionally. A place where the attention was focused on me. A place where I was calm and not worried or anxious about anything. A place where I was totally care-free. This was the only place where I felt completely relaxed. This really speaks volumes about the level of neglect I felt at home. Most people, if not all, have major anxiety about hospitals. I would be remiss if I said I didn't have anxiety about a surgery going wrong, especially with the amount of anxiety that existed within me on a daily basis and the anxiety that was projected onto me. The most amazing thing about going to and being in a hospital, regardless of which surgery I was having, was a feeling of complete relaxation and being completely anxiety-free. Even after I had my second child, the doctor asked if I wanted to stay an extra day…I asked for two days. Most people cannot wait to get out of the hospital. I was never that person. However, being as old as I am now, the COVID pandemic, and now being in a marriage filled with love, I highly doubt I would be as comfortable and willing to be in a hospital today.

So, I had my first surgery, and I was in what seemed to be a tremendous ward with more than a dozen beds all lined up against the wall on both sides of the room. They were all empty except for my bed. I remember, after my surgery, waking up in the middle of the night and seeing my aunt. I thought, great, she came to visit me. When I told my parents that she was here, they totally denied it. They told me she was not. I know what I saw and heard. I thought maybe they didn't want me to be happy that I had a visitor, but it wasn't that. It was only a few years ago that I read that ether can make you hallucinate, and that was the anesthesia that was given to me. This hallucination was a representation of my unconscious need to feel being cared for; therefore, it projected an image of my aunt.

My father's sister, my aunt, was my godmother, and I felt she was a caring figure in my life as opposed to my mother. I realize now that it was the only time in my life I was "high" and probably why I understood my psychotic patients so well when I worked on a psych unit decades later. My experience of a hallucination would enable me to have an experiential understanding of patients.

But why was my mother so afraid to show emotion? I always wondered what made her such a cold human being. Those emotions were in there, and, unfortunately for everyone in the family, that is where she kept them, deep inside of herself. Her life must have been so traumatic for her that she was unable to let those emotions out. I believe if she had allowed herself to feel and allowed others in, she might have feared really losing control and breaking down to a point at which she would not be able to recover.

Chapter 9

HOW I BECAME FLUENT IN LUNACY

"Sticks and stones will break my bones, but words will never hurt me." Yeah, bite me! Broken bones heal. Emotional abuse and neglect can stay with us forever. When I worked in a battered women's shelter, the women unanimously would say the bruises disappear, the broken bones heal, but there is nothing to erase the years of emotional trauma.

Parents are among the most influential role models and we learn all the good and all the bad from them. Hopefully, as we grow and mature, we can throw out most of the bad and keep most of the good. There are no perfect parents. We are human and imperfect. We make mistakes. The best anyone can hope for is that we learn from our experiences and change our behavior.

My early years in elementary school were tough. I went to kindergarten when I was four and three-quarters. The youngest in the class. I could not wait to go to school. I am not sure why. Maybe to get away from my mother. It was a real approach/avoidance issue or shall I say, a disorganized attachment disorder due to the emotional inconsistency exhibited by my parents. I must have felt unloved even at that young age, as I could not wait to get away from her but also missed her at the same time. And my ambivalence was obvious early on. Such ambivalent behavior is characteristic of disorganized attachment disorder.

When I was in first grade, I had trouble reading. I was in the slowest reading group. I suspect my mother didn't spend much time trying to teach me how to read and I have no recollection of my father helping me; the man who read three books a week. One day the teacher called my mother in and told her that if I didn't improve my reading skills, I would be left back. Well, in my head that was not going to happen. I was not going to be ridiculed for getting left back. Getting left back was taboo. No one was going to tell me that I was staying behind. So, I did the only thing I could possibly do. Three months before the end of the school year, I started reading and got promoted to the second grade. Maybe Dick, Jane, and Spot were not exciting enough for me, because, even today, I cannot read something that I am not interested in. This incident was one of the earliest signs of my rebellion, my survival skills, and my obstinance that stayed with me for the rest of my life. It's an example of my resilience. I have no explanation why I was slow at reading or why I chose not to read at a higher level, but I can say I was always oppositional. My rebelliousness was and currently is a defense to protect myself from criticism—it simply cuts the criticism off just like my mother cut off her emotions. Obviously, my mother was a singular positive role model in this respect. She taught me how to protect myself!

When I was in the third grade, the class was not listening to the teacher, and the teacher said, "One more word from anyone and the class gets homework." Of course, I said out loud, "Word," and yes, the class was not happy with me. I always tested the limits, pushed the envelope, and did not like the feeling of being controlled or being told what to do. It was transference. Transference is when a person redirects some of their feelings for one person onto an entirely different person. Clearly, I redirected my rebellious behavior from my mother onto my teacher because I felt controlled. Anyone who behaved like my mother, had power over me, or controlled me in any way, I would rebel against. And for some reason I was not afraid to do so. Maybe it's genetics. Remember when my great-grandmother stood up to the Mafia guy and called him out because he couldn't break the chicken's neck? I was also very much used to getting punished and yelled at, or maybe it was the negative attention I was used to getting. In my head, it did not matter. I would get punished anyway. So why not rebel? This early behavior came in handy later on in life when I became a clinical social worker and had to deal with insurance companies that, at times, refused to pay for services.

But these ingredients were not a good recipe for relationships. I had few friends. I had difficulty making and keeping friends. I blame myself for that. I can honestly say, I am not sure whether I should take the blame, considering kids can be cruel, but I do feel responsible for having difficulty with relationships. After all, I am the common denominator. I did have a good friend up until the third or fourth grade. Her name was Ruth. We had the same lunch-box and at times would grab the wrong one at the end of the day. I would take hers home and she would take mine home. But we were friends. I think we gravitated toward one another because we were both shy and on some level, outcasts. Unfortunately, she had to move in the middle of the school year because her mom died. After that, I felt alone. I had no one to hang out with or talk to. I could not connect with anyone; I was not cut out to have a "friend group." I could not manage being in a group. That was too overwhelming for me. Especially knowing what the group was like that I lived with, I could only imagine what strangers would be like.

I would come home from school upset, with no one to talk to at lunchtime and feeling that no one liked me. But how could anyone like me?—my parents didn't like me. I was not a happy kid and was not fun to be around. I was also my mother's child. In many ways, just like her. How can anyone connect to someone if her parent was unable to connect to her? I was needy and clingy. I was made fun of.

I was born with club feet. As an infant, I was in a plastic cast for several months to straighten my feet. The cast would be removed at night when I slept. I then had to wear corrective shoes for years, which made me more of a target for being ridiculed. In school, I had to wear these hideous, corrective, orthopedic shoes. Here I was a young kid wearing these red, unstylish, old lady shoes, seeming much bulkier than the "normal" shoes kids my age would wear. This added another layer of anxiety to my life. At the time, I had no conscious understanding of the significance of wearing corrective shoes. There was always a feeling of uneasiness when I was at school. I felt helpless and hopeless, different and odd with no support and no one at home to empathize or comfort me about the criticism I was exposed to at school. It was never explained to me that there would be consequences later on in life if I didn't wear these shoes and that my feet would never be "normal." I remember someone asking me why I wore those shoes and if I really liked them. I recall just staring at her. It might have been the fifth or sixth grade when I was finally able to wear normal, stylish shoes for the first time and not go to a special store to buy my shoes. It felt wonderful. I no longer felt odd or abnormal. I felt as if I fit in with the other kids; even if I was not part of the "in crowd," it still felt good. As I got older, I would wear open-toed shoes and would only wear shoes when I had to. As an adult, I usually go barefoot whenever I can. So, when my daughter got married in the summer, I wore stylish, glittered, flip-flops to the wedding. As an aside, when my daughter was born, she wore corrective shoes as an infant for several months. Genetics is the gift that keeps on giving. As much as I have almost perfect feet now (I have been told I have beautiful feet by whomever does my pedicure), I am grateful that my parents, at least, took care of my feet. Even though my parents took care of my problematic feet, it had an emotional impact on me that has lingering effects to this day.

After my only friend moved away, it was decided that Dominic would talk to my teacher and have the teacher "assign" friends to me. I am not sure if it was my brother's idea (being the middle child, the peacemaker) or my mother's. However, it was so humiliating, forcing kids to be my friend. I remember one kid volunteered to be my friend, but honestly, I am not sure how well that worked out, as I must have blocked that out of my head.

Not having many friends, basically only one or two at a time, I never had to approach my mother about having anyone over to the house. Honestly, I was never comfortable having anyone over, as I was always under surveillance. I must have been around twelve when for the first time, I wanted my friend to come over to my house. I sheepishly asked my mom if a friend could come over. I remember the butterflies in my stomach, the anticipatory anxiety of what she would say. Do I dare ask her or just suffer the usual disappointment and shame of not being worthy of having a friend come over? Or, maybe, not feeling worthy enough of having a friend! After pondering this for a day or two and role-playing in my head as to *why* I would possibly want to impose on my mother by having a friend over, I posed the question to her. My hands were sweaty, my heart was pounding. What if she says no? But as I role-played in my head, as a young child, I felt I was prepared. I could hear her say: "Why do you need a friend to come here when you have your brother and sister and friends in the neighborhood to play with? Can't you occupy yourself? I'm too busy to watch over another child! I just cleaned the house! Don't you have enough games to keep yourself busy? Can't you watch TV?" But I had my answers. "I need a break from my siblings and neighborhood kids. I want someone else to play with. She will not be a problem. We will be out of your hair. We will not dirty the house. We will be outside in the pool and there are all reruns on TV now." But there was one thing that never entered my mind. My mother told me she was not allowed in the house. She was not allowed to use the bathroom. How could I have not thought of that or come up with an answer? I felt blindsided. I said "OK" in the hope that my friend would go to the bathroom before she left her house and not have to use our bathroom. I decided I would not offer her any snacks or anything to drink. And, so, my friend came over. We had a great time. We were in the pool, we stayed outside, and everything was going well *until* she had to use the bathroom. I froze and I could feel myself panicking. I could feel all my organs jiggling inside of me, pressing on my bladder and feeling as if I had to pee. I could feel the blood gushing through my arteries to my heart and asking myself, "Am I having a heart attack?" How do I tell my friend that no one is allowed in the house, not even to use the bathroom? Especially the bathroom, as that was a room that was completely sanitized and sterilized. The paper seal over the toilet, which read "sanitized for your protection," would be broken. If she used the bathroom, I would have to check to make sure nothing was out of place before my mother inspected it. No tissues in the garbage pail, the sink had to be wiped clean, and the towels had to be folded just right on the towel bar. But I could not have my only friend not use the bathroom. I knew my enemy, my mother, and knew what to expect. I was unable to predict what the repercussions would be if my friend went back to school and told everyone. I decided the right thing to do was to let her use the bathroom. Looking back, I do not believe anything bad happened to me. My memory is not that clear; therefore, I have to assume I did not get in trouble. I would have remembered. But when I think about the unnecessary anxiety my mother created for me and how ridiculous the entire situation was, I just have to shake my head. Luckily, when I'm in a hotel and I see the paper seal on the toilet in the bathroom, I am not triggered.

Dominic was allowed to have friends over with no questions asked, no rules, no limitations. Trish never had friends over when she was in high school. However, once she was out of school and working, that changed. The only conclusion I can come up with is that I was being punished for my own existence. For just being. For just being born. But if this experience taught me anything, it taught me one thing. Be prepared, at all times. I must think of everything. I must always have my ducks in a row; rows going beyond the orchestra seats and way up into the balcony. I cannot leave anything to chance. I must be three steps ahead of everyone. Anticipate the unanticipated! Having all my ducks in a row almost allows me to control my anxiety. This was a lesson learned for a lifetime. Quack, quack, quack!

As I reflect on this incident at the age of sixty-eight, I feel I am at a loss for words. The lunacy, the insanity of her behavior, the anxiety and emotional abuse that was inflicted upon me, are, on some level, unspeakable. It now gives me a much better understanding as to why I only have one true friend. I was never socialized in a fashion that would enable me to interact with people easily.

Surprisingly, going to college as an adult not only gave me book smarts but also an education in life. I was no longer sheltered, and college exposed me to diversity, cultures, and others' experiences, allowing me to be open and empathic toward others. It afforded me the opportunity to escape from the lunacy bin that I had been exposed to growing up.

Chapter 10

I ALWAYS WANTED TO BECOME A HAIRSTYLIST, BUT MY MOM SAID I DIDN'T HAVE THE PERSONALITY TO DEAL WITH PEOPLE, SO I BECAME A PSYCHOTHERAPIST INSTEAD

I got through elementary school and went on to junior high school. The junior high school was in the same building as the high school. There were four wings jutting out of the main corridor of the school. The first wing was for the junior high and the other three wings were for the high school students. The school was built in 1957, and by the time I attended classes there, the school was still quite new. The school had a boys gym and a girls gym. The girls gym was about half the size of the boys gym, mainly because the boys gym had bleachers that pulled out for rallies and basketball games. The school had a football field, tennis courts, baseball field, and a huge field that was used for lacrosse and for gym classes when it was warm enough to go outside.

Kids were tough back in the late sixties and early seventies. School did not get any easier. Not only were boys fighting with each other but girls were also beating each other up. I was not one of those cool kids, and I made sure I kept my head down. I was able, or had to, keep my oppositional behavior in check and my mouth shut if I did not want to get beat up and, literally, survive high school. I valued keeping my body safe and intact more than being oppositional. I was not stupid in that way. I was terrified of pissing off the wrong person. But that didn't mean I did not screw up once or twice.

When I was in high school, I remember being in the girls locker room of the gym. There was a girl who I knew, who knew my neighbor, and my neighbor was kind of dorky. We were talking in the locker room and I, jokingly, told her I thought she liked my neighbor. She objected to that comment. She was a rather large person, more than twice my size. I was maybe ninety pounds and five foot seven at the time. Well, she literally picked me up and threw me against the lockers. I suddenly found myself airborne at a speed that seemed faster than light while simultaneously slow as shit. All I remember seeing were the black and gray padlocks and the gray lockers whizzing past me, as I was tossed against the lockers like a salad. It seemed so easy for her to pick me up and fling me without any thought behind it. I remember thinking, if I get hurt, how do I explain this to my mother? I knew my mother would be taking down names and phone numbers and that would be another humiliation, another battle I would have to face in school the next day. I can hear my father's voice saying, "I know people." Luckily, the only thing injured was my ego, even though I was a bit sore. But I became even quieter after that. Most importantly, I had learned a lesson from my mother years before. She would say, "Stop crying or I will give you something to cry about." From that point on, I became even tougher. That was the day I stopped crying. I held in my tears for decades to come. She wanted me to stifle my emotions the way she stifled her own emotions. It would be forty years before I cried again. It was when my sister died, and I only cried privately. That baffles my current husband because he cries at a dog food commercial.

The entire four years of high school I had a few friends, and their friends became my friends. We were a pretty tight group that stayed tight until graduation. But I hated school. My GPA was extremely low, and if I had to attend an additional year of high school, I probably would have dropped out. I hated being institutionalized, the ritual, the obedience, the control, and the kids I could not stand; the kids I was afraid of.

What I did learn to do was to spice it up a bit to make school more bearable. Once a month on a Friday morning in my senior year of high school, we would cut the first period and go out for breakfast. I had money because my mother told me at the age of fourteen or fifteen to "go get a job and don't come home until you have one." So, who do kids go to when they have a problem? I went directly to my friends who were already working at a factory on an assembly line putting plastic toys together. They told me to call the manager, and they assured me I would be hired. And I was. Little did I know that my mother would want part of my income and that I would have to pay rent. She took 50 percent of my pay. I made twenty dollars a week and she took ten dollars. She told me I had to pay for my own clothes, pay for the hot lunch at school, and any additional entertainment I may want to partake in. Even though she did continue to buy my clothes. But I learned the value of a dollar.

Since I was one of the youngest in my class, most of my friends were driving already. On a Friday morning, we would all hop into someone's car and go out for breakfast. The attendance person at the school, when I think back on it, was probably pretty stupid or didn't care, as she never caught on that this was a monthly thing to miss the first-period class. I learned how to forge my mother's signature so there were never any consequences for being late. I also learned how to drive when I was sixteen, which was illegal back then. My friends had no problem with anyone getting behind the wheel of their cars, so by the time I got my driver's permit, I was a fairly experienced driver.

But it was my father who actually taught me how to drive and I considered him to be an excellent driver. I got my permit on my seventeenth birthday, which is in December. I learned how to drive in the snow and that was fun. We lived at the bottom of a hill. A hill we would sleigh-ride down in the winter. One day my dad took me out driving and took me down a snow-covered side street. There were hardly any cars on that road. We were stopped on top of the hill. He directed me to drive down the hill and slam on the brakes. When I think back, it was pretty brave of my father to be in a car with an inexperienced driver and give me those instructions. I followed his directions. I skidded and swerved and finally came to a stop. It was kind of fun actually. He said, "Did you see what just happened? Don't ever do that again, as you will cause an accident." I was confused and thought, "Then why did you tell me to do such a thing?" At that point, he taught me how to steer into the skid to maintain control of the car. To this day, I love driving in the snow. This was one of the few times I actually spent quality time with my father.

When I was a junior in high school, I started dating this guy. He had already graduated. He was older than me, but that was not the issue for my mother. The issue was that his parents were divorced, and she didn't want me to be with him. Being from a "broken home" was taboo. Divorce was taboo despite the fact that she had two sisters who were divorced. One night, I told my mother I was going out with my friends and I met up with him. She caught me in a lie; somehow, moms always know when their kids are up to no good. Except my mother was so far up my ass that when I yawned, you could see her glaring face. My mother was the analogue of LoJack. When I got home, she told me she had called my friends looking for me. I never felt or thought my friends ratted me out. I believe they were just as afraid of my mother as I was. My punishment was that my mother refused to attend my junior ring ceremony. Additionally, she took the phone out of my room, and I was the only one in the house with a separate phone line. I was grounded for God knows how long. But the only thing that was truly painful was that neither of my parents attended my junior ring ceremony, which meant so much to me. To this day, I still do not understand how she could have been so punitive. I had tried to tell myself it was her loss, not mine, but that provided little comfort. The emotional consequence was always worse and long-lasting. Dominic attended the ceremony. He was the only one. My sister refused to attend. Needless to say, the relationship with the guy ended soon after that.

Growing up, I was punished a lot. My mother had a very punitive streak toward me. This only applied to me though. Being punctual was a rule that was very important to my mother when it came to me, not to my brother or sister, but just to me. If I was, no exaggeration, two minutes late, I was punished. Grounded and the phone taken away. This has had an effect on me that has lasted a lifetime as I am never late for anything. I am always early. The consequence of this was twofold. First, the positive consequence is that my children could always count on me. They know if I say I will be there at two they can expect me at one thirty. The negative consequence occurred when I worked in the hospital and I had to punch a time clock in and out daily. One day I got called down to administration. They told me I was not allowed to hang around the time clock to punch in and out. I was totally confused and puzzled at what they were talking about, so I questioned what they meant by that. They told me I punch in and out at the exact same time every day. Again, puzzled, I asked them what they were talking about. They said, again, you are not allowed to hang around the time clock. I said I don't do that, and they asked me to explain why I punch in and out at the same time every day. I told them it was a pathology from childhood and something that I was unable to change. I told them that I would always be at my desk earlier than expected and would leave the hospital when my shift ends. I told them this was something that cannot be fixed. I could not change this behavior. I left the administrative offices and that was the last I heard about it.

I was so terrified of my mother that, to this day, if I am late, I go into a panic and believe someone will be upset with me and there will be a negative consequence. If I am late, I become extremely anxious and have difficulty functioning. My sister, on the other hand, was the opposite. Trish was late for everything, and my mother tolerated it. The joke was that she would be late for her own funeral. Ha, I made sure that did not happen; her funeral ran on time. Trish had a very different attitude. She would refer to my mother as "shadow traffic." That phrase was on the local news when the helicopters would fly above NYC and report traffic, back in the late sixties and early seventies. One day Trish was a few minutes late coming home from work and my mother was frantic. When she arrived home five minutes late, my mom immediately said, "Why couldn't you call to tell me you were going to be late?" (No cell phones back then). Trish, who did not give a shit, was so laid back most of the time that you had to put a mirror under her nose to see if she was breathing, said, expressionless, "There was a red light."

I don't ever remember my brother getting punished and my sister rarely went out of the house. Dominic would come home and tell my parents that he was driving one hundred miles an hour on Route 80 or that he smoked pot or he would come home drunk. Not a problem, no consequence. Life is good when you're Italian with a penis! There were never any consequences for him, and I'm sure that was a decision made by my father. It was not my mother's decision, but she would never question my father when it came to Dominic. Since my brother was a little kid, my dad feared he would become gay, probably because he was surrounded by women. Two sisters and lots of girls in the neighborhood. His ignorance was obvious by his belief that one can just switch sides due to the company one keeps. Therefore, my brother could do no wrong, my sister never did anything wrong, and I was the "normal teenager" who just wanted to fit in. And being a "normal teenager" was something my parents were unable to handle, especially since I am female.

I remember buying my first pair of bell-bottom pants. My dad called me a "whore," probably thinking that would keep me in line. But it had the opposite effect. Being oppositional or rebellious, his comment only made me go out and buy more bell bottoms. My mother also called me a whore as an adult once, in public, at my house in front of lots of company. My ex's cousin came to me privately the moment it happened because she was so appalled that a mother would criticize her daughter like that in front of so many people. She told me my mother called me a whore because she found out that I smoked *once*. When I was a young child and was in the car with my mom and my aunt, I witnessed my mom puffing on a cigarette. I wonder if my mother saw herself as a whore. Did she feel bad about herself for smoking? Whatever she felt, she projected onto me. I also wonder how she felt about her sisters who smoked too.

This is how I learned to be thick-skinned and be able to walk away from people. My being oppositional and rebellious helped me to survive. I did not cave or knuckle under. I was not silenced. It was a portrayal of my resilience. It allowed me to survive. I became hypervigilant at an early age and was able to tune in to controlling people. It was my family that labeled me "troubled and oppositional." Oppositional was not something my therapists have described or diagnosed me as having. It was all anxiety and attachment issues. I believe it was very difficult for my mother to see me having fun, probably because, I assume, she never had fun growing up. Having fun had to be done in secret. Another taboo.

When I was sixteen and Dominic was seventeen, there was talk about where Dominic was going to go to college. There was no plan for me or my sister because our futures were already planned, although my sister did go to community college for a semester. The plan for me and my sister was to work in an office as secretaries, be slaves to men, especially at that time, and find a husband to support us. My sister answered phones throughout her entire working life until she passed.

In my senior year of high school, I would go to school for half a day and work in an office the rest of the day. At that time, I would do anything to get out of school, and working and making money was empowering, giving me a sense of independence. I always had a very good work ethic, mainly because I was taught to obey. But this career path was not my choice. I told my mother that I wanted to be a hairstylist. I loved fixing my hair and I always had the latest hairstyles. Had my hair long and short, and tried all the different haircuts. I was not afraid of how it would look or afraid of what others may think. I just did it. My hair was everything to me. The only thing my mother would not let me do as a teenager was to dye my hair. But at the age of sixteen, this is what I wanted to do with my life.

When it came time for me to have the conversation with my mother as to my career path, I should not have been surprised at what she said, but, then again, I was. I always held on to the hope that, someday, my mother would support me. I told my mother I wanted to become a hairstylist, as it was a real passion of mine at that time. Her goal for me was very different. She wanted me to work in an office like she did when she was younger. Her response was something, once again, unexpected. She told me I would never succeed as a hairstylist because "You don't have the personality to deal with people." If this was my choice, I would have to pay for it because she was not going to pay for me to go to beauty school. I never went to my dad to see if he would pay for it, primarily because I figured he would agree with my mom. I was, however, very disappointed and upset, and felt I had no other option but to work in an office. When I think about her words today, I shake my head and laugh. I was unable to become a hairstylist "because" I did not have the personality to deal with people, so decades later I decided to become a psychotherapist.

My mother never had a choice about what she wanted to do, and she made sure that I did not have a choice either. What was even more infuriating was that my father paid for Dominic's education and for Trish to attend a semester at a community college. And I, sadly, never had a choice about what I wanted to do, just like my mother never had a choice. There were no options on the table for me.

Chapter 11

"MY MOTHER WAS LIKE RADIATION, I DIDN'T FEEL THE EFFECTS TILL YEARS LATER"

—ROSEANNE BARR

Actions speak louder than words; however, in my house even the words were forbidden. The difference was my siblings did get the actions. My siblings had my parents' emotional support, as little as it was, regardless of what they wanted to do. The punishments were less severe or non existent for them compared to me. What they were unable to get from my mother, they got from my father. I received nothing from either of them.

It was not until decades later, decades of therapy and analytic training, that I could look back and understand my own behavior. My mother's lack of control over her own life, the trauma of being a child of the Great Depression, and whatever trauma she might have experienced that I will never know about, all of this lack of control was projected onto me. This projection, in theory, was primarily a reaction to having a child she did not want. She was unable to come to terms with being pregnant, again, with me. She felt she had no outlet for processing her emotions with my father about being pregnant. If the act of conceiving me was not a forced act and she welcomed the sex, then she would have to be totally responsible for the pregnancy. Either way, she could never admit to this "accident" or be responsible for this pregnancy. Her ego was too fragile. She had to oppress me, and that oppression resulted in punishing me. This oppression made me rebellious. She produced in me the exact behavior she wanted to prevent. Her jealousy of me being strong-willed infuriated her, and that's why she punished me. She was not able to rebel. We were locked into a perpetual battle of wills.

My mother's behavior toward me had lasting effects. My mother was not consistent with her love. I was afraid of the person from whom I was seeking care and love. I had low self-esteem, lots of anxiety, and major trust issues. I found myself going through many relationships, both romantic with men and friendships with women. Life seemed somewhat chaotic at times and I didn't understand why. I was always told it was me and my attitude. There was this constant feeling of not being good enough and being unlovable. I hated myself for a long time. I had become a reflection of my mother. I was a carbon copy of my mother. I had her anxiety, her low self-esteem, and her mistrust of the universe. I didn't like her, so how could I possibly like myself? This is classic attachment disorder. However, I have never been officially diagnosed, and if it was a diagnosis, I was never told. There is only one difference between me and my mother. She needed approval from everyone. I am not motivated by someone's approval of me. Because of my parents' attitude toward me, I became very thick-skinned. If someone does not like me, I am not affected the way my mother was affected. I bury those feelings, deny them. However, burying these feelings is not healthy, but it was the only way I was able to survive. I lived a life of seeking my parents' approval, which is not unusual. Most people want their parents' approval. That approval was impossible to achieve.

A parent's approval of their child should begin when the child is born. If it is not there from the start and the parent does not adjust their behavior and show love toward the child, that child will never get that parent's approval. I learned that it is not worth my energy to win someone over. My mother was like radiation, I did not feel the effects till years later. And it is at that time when one must take a look at themselves and decide if they want to change certain behaviors. For me, my life started to change when I was in my early thirties, due to my own initiative.

My mother was not emotionally present for any of us. But no one ever spoke about it. We would joke about Mom's behavior, but it was all superficial. My siblings, especially my sister, seldom said anything negative about my mother. Even as adults, I was the lone rebel, as they were still too dependent and afraid of her to go against her. My siblings never wanted to hear anything negative about her. We would make jokes about her behavior, but nothing that ever turned into a substantial conversation. I needed to vent to both of them. I thought they would understand and validate my feelings. But I received no validation. They were not going there.

My early experience laid the foundation that underscored my relationship with my first husband, a relationship in which I unconsciously attempted to fix my mother. Some of us marry someone very similar to the parent we have the most difficulty with in an attempt to fix the parent by fixing the spouse. If we can fix the spouse, we can fix the parent. Of course, this is all unconscious—and *never* works. I married my mother the first time around. Unfortunately, I did not have access to a Geiger counter to detect the radiation that was being emitted by my first husband.

Chapter 12

LEAVING MY MOTHER AND BRINGING HER ALONG; TOO MANY PEOPLE IN THE BED

The transition from leaving my mother's home and entering married life was complicated. You cannot run away from your problems; they always follow you. Problems require processing, dissecting, understanding, and a change in perception before someone can move forward and not repeat old behaviors. As much as I looked forward to escaping from my mother, her tentacles continued to strangle me, and, emotionally, she was always within me. Unconsciously, as I pursued Oscar, what I was really doing was preparing for an intervention. Oscar was the proxy for my mother. I was rebooting my primary relationship. And once again, when technology works, it is great, but when technology goes south… However, in my head, this was my chance to start over. I would now be able to stand my ground. I probably was delusional. I was going to redefine my primary relationship. I would re-create myself in that I would no longer be a victim. I would have a voice. I would be able to assert myself, my independence. However, the bed was too crowded. My mother's voice did not leave me, and I became even more smothered, becoming sandwiched between my husband and my mother.

I approached my marriage with a positive outlook. I was extremely naïve and was very much in love. In retrospect, I now, having benefited from therapy, can see "that emotion of love" blinded me. Now I know, I was innocently drawn in. He was "familiar," and I unconsciously thought I would be able to manage this relationship. After all, I was fluent in lunacy and developed certain techniques to survive that type of relationship. Foolishly, I thought that I would do more than merely survive; in this new relationship, I thought I would thrive. I was so blinded by love that the tentacles actually felt like an embrace.

Chapter 13

WHAT WAS THIS YOUNG, NAÏVE, SHELTERED WOMAN THINKING?–SHE WASN'T, BUT LOVE IS BLIND

The psychological process that transpired in the marriage was something that was experienced as unique to me but occurs in many relationships. After years of treatment, becoming educated, and doing post grad work at an analytic institute, I realized that Oscar and my mother were one and the same. I realized why I was drawn to him. It is never just one person's fault for the failure or success of a relationship. My description of my marriage is intended to depict what transpired between the two of us based on *my* experience and *my* perception of the relationship. It is based on how my relationship with my mother unconsciously influenced my decision to choose the person I did to be my partner.

I graduated from high school and the part-time job I had worked at while I was in high school offered me a full-time position. My neighbor said he could get me a job where he worked; bigger company, better benefits and pay, and opportunity for advancement. I went on the interview and was hired on the spot. Back in the day, résumés were not required, and for someone applying for clerical work, it was easy to be hired immediately.

I had a job as a receptionist. I greeted visitors, answered phones, and typed. I worked beside a woman whom I had difficulty getting along with; transference, my mother. This woman's personality was similar to my mother's. However, I guess I am not surprised that I was unable to get along with her, since I was told I'm not good with people.

The typing I did was for those not high up enough on the corporate ladder to have their own "private" secretaries. They would bring their work to me, and I would do their typing. One person in particular caught my eye.

There was a young man I became attracted to. He was tall, had a good appearance, but was not necessarily well-proportioned. He had a sense of humor, not a jokester but more tongue in cheek. He was a quick-witted type of person, with lots of sarcasm. He was educated and well-informed about world events. He was a real go-getter, ambitious, and eager to climb the corporate ladder.

And here I was, seventeen years old, five feet seven inches tall, dark brown hair, and brown eyes with a body type only to be described as lean. Some would say under-nourished, skin and bones, as I was barely ninety pounds soaking wet. I would hear comments that I was too thin, thin as a thread. But my slender figure was not deliberate, there was no eating disorder. I lived in a state of constant anxiety, which, I believe, contributed to having a fast metabolism which prevented me from gaining weight even if I tried (if only that were true today). One can also throw in the genetic component. However, Oscar was never impressed with my body. Like my mother, compliments weren't his forte and he never hesitated to tell me what was wrong with me.

I eventually became his secretary. We were attracted to one another and started dating. I quit that job shortly after we started dating. As a matter of fact, I went through a series of jobs when I worked as a secretary. I believe I was hoping to find a company that I really liked. I had a history of going from job to job, staying several months to a year at each company. It wasn't a matter of finding the right job, it was a matter of finding the right career. I hated working in an office. It wasn't my choice to work in an office, it was my mother's decision. I was a good typist but not a good stenographer. My high school stenography teacher told me never to tell any prospective employer I could take steno. I just was not good at it.

Oscar and I continued to date after I left the company, which was probably better for our relationship. But we were both on the rebound. His relationship had ended before mine did. I had ended my relationship after I started working for the company and before we started dating.

My mother was head over heels for Oscar. She thought he had money because he bought a brand-new car shortly after we started dating. Whenever she blinked, she saw dollar signs on the inside of her eyelids. She saw me in a wedding dress and out of the house. She envisioned him taking care of me for the rest of *her* life and thinking she would finally be rid of me. The message I got from my mother since I was a teen was the following: "You must find a man and get married. In order to do that you must have a smile on your face all the time and never show a man you're upset or angry. A man does not want to be with a woman who is not smiling and does not look pretty." *Wow*, the pressure! The problem here was that I was not a happy person. Neither was my mother, so I wonder how she was able to land my father.

Once Oscar came into the picture, my mother became less strict with me. I assume she did not want to screw up this relationship by showing him what a bitch she really was to me. I was able to stay out later than ten o'clock and was no longer punished for coming home two minutes late. It was obvious she wanted Oscar to stick around. If he stuck around, she knew, sooner or later, I would not be sticking around and eventually would marry him.

We dated for about a year and got engaged on Valentine's Day. We set a date for the fall of that same year. We got married shortly before my twentieth birthday. But love is blind, and I was stupid. I believed things would change and be better. I ignored some significant signs and red flags. I loved him, but I was too young and too innocent.

He had a large family and he had similar issues with his mother, as I had with my mother. However, he never recognized his mother as being an issue. He needed his family's approval, especially from his mother. He needed to be needed and needed to always call the shots and be in control. There was also something that did not register with me until years after we divorced. I was aware of it, was angry about it, but was blinded by the big bright red flag that constantly waved in the breeze outside my bedroom window. And to say it was a breeze is an underestimate. It was more like gale-force winds. During our courtship, the only time we went out to dinner alone was the night we got engaged. All the other times, he would invite other people to join us, at the last minute. At that time, I had no understanding as to why that happened.

When I think about this today, I believe he must have felt threatened by me. Most likely, I was a trigger for him. A potentially powerful woman with whom he might have to struggle for approval. He always told me that I became powerful when I was angry. The evidence for my being a trigger could be the following. I had a *big* mouth with an ungenerous filter. He was so fearful of being publicly embarrassed that he needed the protective arsenal provided by the additional dinner guests.

In the beginning, I found his family to be fun and wild. I was used to a large extended family but not a large immediate family. They would gather sometimes on a weekly basis at someone's house and stay to the wee hours of the night. What that actually meant was no one wanted to be the first one to leave the party because once you were gone, they would talk about you. It was exhausting for me because I was working and keeping house; I would go to bed very early and rise very early. And saying goodbye to his family was also an hourlong ordeal. But it did not matter, because how I felt was never a concern for him. There were many things I didn't know about him until we were married for a long time, and I'm sure it was the same for him.

When we got engaged, my father sat me down and proceeded to tell me the following: "If you are serious about this wedding, you better put your money where your mouth is. *You* will be paying for half of this wedding and I will pay for the other half." I have no recollection of what I felt or thought. I was too stupid to argue and maybe a bit scared to confront him. But I can tell you *now* what I think. What the hell? He made no attempt to pay for college for me, not that I was interested in higher education at that time. That option was not on the table for me, like it was for Dominic. But the offer to pay for beauty school was not even in his head. I never approached him about becoming a hairstylist because I knew my mother had the last word. As a matter of fact, he paid for nothing for me that was over and above what he legally had to pay for: food, clothing, shelter, and the cars that he gave us. In addition, my mother told me who was going to be my maid of honor—my sister. I had no choice in the matter. I wanted to have one of my friends stand up for me and have my sister as a bridesmaid. I was never that close with my sister. I was closer to my friends than my sister. But that decision was taken from me. It was not the worst thing; it was more about not having control.

But there was so much evidence of how the rules differed for me compared to my siblings. When my sister got married, it was my understanding that she had to pay half for her wedding also. After my parents passed and I was going through their stuff, much to my surprise (and I am not sure why I am always surprised), I found evidence that my dad had not been truthful with me. My dad kept records of everything, just like the Germans did during the Holocaust. And the way the Germans had their day in court, so did my father, except he was already dead when I found out what he had done. As I went through his records, and his records were impeccably detailed, he listed the monetary wedding gift he gave my sister. As an aside, my father had personal financial information on both my sister and brother, but nothing on me, as if he only had two children.

As I read over his ledger, my eyes suddenly became engulfed with flames to the point I could feel the heat throughout my body. I was now in a desert, my mouth was dry, feeling like cotton balls, I was dehydrating, with no way to irrigate the drought that resided inside my body. There was no way to extinguish the burning sensation that consumed me. My parents continued to hurt me even from the grave, and the emotional turmoil that I thought I had buried was again resurrected. My body started to quiver. My arms and legs began making these jerking movements, as my breathing became labored. My hands were shaking as I stared into space, thinking I was going to lose consciousness. I thought I was having a seizure. The physical discomfort then changed to anger. The steam began bursting out of my ears, like a volcanic fissure, allowing an eruption of lava to explode in my head. I could smell the stench of sulfuric acid penetrating and burning my nostrils, the heat traveling through my body from my head down to my toes, as the sweat flowed over me like Niagara Falls. There was so much

Diane Harth

steam exiting through my ears, I thought the moisture and fog would engulf my house. I thought I would suffocate. The strength that overpowered me, as the adrenaline rushed through my body, gave me the sense that I probably had the capacity to break the hardcover of the ledger in half with my bare hands, as I tore that page out of his ledger. It was unbearable seeing that page in his ledger. I was in disbelief about how someone, not anyone, but my own father could possibly lie to me like that. What could I have done to my father that he would not want to pay for my wedding? The emotional pain was unbearable. I felt sick, dizzy. I started questioning my life, my behavior. Maybe I blocked something out of my memory, something that I did that was so horrendous it stayed in my unconscious for all these years. What did I do that would make my father emotionally hurt me so much? What did I do that would make him lie about this? Was I that much of a burden to him? At that moment, I saw my father as a coward. Was there a reason he gave my sister a wedding gift and not me? And if so, why couldn't he tell me and be honest?

There was nothing I could have done at that point, and as I started to process what I found in his ledger, I realized there was a silver lining in all this. I was strong because of this. I was the only one of his three children who knew how to manage money, who was independent, and was able to survive on their own.

However, very late in life, just before he went into assisted living, he said to me, "The worst decision I ever made in my life was to have kids." What he *actually* meant was, the worst decision he ever made was to have *me*, because my brother told me that my father told him the opposite. He told Dominic the best decision he ever made was to have kids. It is really amazing what one finds out after the parents die. And that is a lesson I've learned. I refuse to lie to my kids, regardless of how painful the truth is. They always know exactly where their mother stands.

My wedding day arrived, and my mom woke me up at seven that morning. She was very excited about my day. She was so excited that to me, it almost felt like she was the one getting married. And then the most ridiculous, asinine words came out of my mother's mouth. It was nineteen years too late, but we finally had the sex talk, which should have happened years ago, but it was not the talk I had expected. She said, "Tonight will be your wedding night, make like you enjoy it." And then she said the unthinkable. And why am I surprised? She said to me, "After you say 'I do,' you can *never* come back to this house to live with me under any circumstances." And my thought was, I will never return to this house again, bitch! Fast-forward a couple of decades down the road, both my sister and brother returned home to live with my parents after their divorces. My brother for a couple of weeks, my sister, however, was there till the day she died. And yes, all three of us got divorced. God, they did a wonderful job of role modeling for us.

The wedding went off without a hitch. Oscar criticized my dress, telling me it did not fit right. I thought it was fine. My mother was a seamstress and I think she would have flung the woman who altered my dress out the window if anything was wrong with it. This was another example of how Oscar was like my mom. Critical, even on our wedding day, when all brides look beautiful. Ironically, that was one of the few days I was not criticized by my mother. It seemed to me they were a tag team.

There was also the controlling part and a "get even" side of Oscar that I was not aware of when we were dating. He refused to tell me where we were going on our honeymoon. Oscar was upset that my parents had so much input when organizing our wedding. He was upset that he was only allowed to invite sixty people to the wedding. This was the seventies. This was customary and traditional. He had no intention of paying for anything, especially for more people to attend the wedding on his side. It's not like he had absolutely no say; he had input on the venue, choosing the menu, and the photographer. The truth is, he was unable to confront his mother and tell her there was a limit to the number of people she could invite. He was afraid of his mother, the way I was afraid of my mother and my father. He, therefore, decided that I would not have any input as to where we would honeymoon. And of course, he spun it to his advantage: "Aren't surprises fun?" Additionally, I found out after we were married that my engagement ring was still not paid for, and he had little to no money for the honeymoon.

Oscar felt controlled and no one likes to be controlled. He felt he had no input into the wedding plans. This feeling of him having no control was a trigger. This was his transference of his mother controlling him. In addition, this gets complicated by his feeling controlled by my parents, who were planning the wedding. But he was just as controlling as my mother, especially when it came to money. Planning the honeymoon without me was a retaliation to regain control over the situation. I had absolutely no say.

He held the purse strings like a pit bull gripping onto someone's leg. He was very cheap. Needless to say, he was thrilled with my Italian family that only gave money at weddings; his family only gave gifts. When I questioned him about spending money on our honeymoon (notice, I said, "When I questioned him," as he never included me in any financial matters), he told me *he* was going to use the money we got from the wedding.

A lack of truthfulness or effective communication with one's partner was what I had experienced in my family. The lack of sharing information was commonplace for me. But I was in love with him and too blind to see the warning signs. I was young, ignorant, and very naïve. As I reflect on that conversation, when I really think about it, I got screwed, and not in a good way. There was no foreplay, no orgasm. I paid for my wedding, my engagement ring, and the honeymoon. Oscar hit the jackpot!

Chapter 14

THE FIRST SEVEN YEARS, DID I BREAK A MIRROR?

Getting married on the thirteenth of the month did not prove to be a lucky number. The honeymoon period did not last very long. We fought a lot and nothing ever really got resolved. It was the same issues over and over again: money and his family. He disliked my family, which I could understand because I felt the same way. However, my family was always there to help us. My family gave, and his family took. His family resembled a tornado except there was no sounding of an alarm to warn me to take shelter, to hide from the violent turbulence that would whisk me into the air and drop me like a water balloon. All of a sudden, the sky would become dark, the barometric pressure would change, and I could feel the violent squall taking over, feeling trapped with no place to take cover. I never knew when it was going to hit, and by the time I could feel the vibrations of the storm rolling in, it was too late. I was unable to mentally prepare myself for his family's intrusion, as I was for my family. If I wanted my marriage to work and in order to survive, I had to readjust my mental compass. I was not prepared for the constant financial support Oscar gave to his parents while he monitored every penny I spent. I was in emotional turmoil, alone in a vat of hollowness, devastation everywhere with no storm cellar to hide in, overwhelmed with everything I was feeling. I wondered when the wind would subside, when the dust would settle in order for me to clean up the emotional mess that was going on in my head. As long as I was married to him, I never felt, within myself, the serenity and safety that one should feel within a marriage.

Two days after we came home from our honeymoon, his mother wanted money. I immediately said, "No," but he was relentless. I told him: "If they can't pay their bills, that is a consequence of their poor money management behavior. We are not responsible for paying their bills." I now understand why he was always short of cash. However, later on in our marriage, he would give money to his family without telling me. Eventually, I would find out, we would fight, and nothing would get resolved. A collection of embers of anger and resentment would begin to form. Like my father, he too was a prisoner of a strong woman.

We lived in an apartment in Saddle Brook, in a two-family house, for about two years, and I had a difficult time adjusting. Our landlady was a crotchety old woman who never gave us enough heat or hot water and complained about everything. I wanted a house in the worst way. I wanted a washer and dryer and a dishwasher. However, our landlady was an old woman living below us, behaving similarly to my mother, constantly telling me what to do.

This was a trigger for me. It seemed impossible for me to escape controlling women.

Oscar avoided doing anything in the apartment, and I was not smart enough to ask him either. I worked all day, came home, cooked, cleaned, and washed clothes at the laundromat. Of course, he did the food shopping, only to control what was being purchased.

I could not wait to move out of the apartment, but Oscar was in graduate school and we had to wait for him to get his degree before we could look for a house. Again, much to my surprise, I had no say as to where we were going to live. His motto for the next twenty years was "I make the money, I make the decisions." And out of the other side of his mouth, he referred to himself as an advocate for women's rights. So, of course, when it came time to buy a house, we moved very close to his family.

I knew practically nothing about our finances, had little interest in knowing, as he handled it all, and I was still very much stuck in "ancient" gender roles. When it came to putting a deposit on the house, he had to ask my father for money. It was several thousand dollars, and we had a verbal contract with him, detailing what we would pay each month and when the loan was to be paid in full. Let me set the scene. If we were a minute late with the payment, my mother would call me to tell me we were late and yell at me, just like when I was a teenager coming home two minutes late. But this time she had little to no power over me and was unable to punish me the way she did when I was a teenager. Oscar was never one for paying bills early and always waited until the last minute. One could say he was "closed-fisted," but I call it being cheap. My mother would never talk to Oscar about the payment, as she held men in "high regard" and she was afraid of upsetting him. She never wanted to confront a man. However, my mother put me in the middle of my father and my husband, creating a conflict for me.

During this time when we owed them money, Oscar bought a new car. My mother went absolutely berserk, and my father demanded that the balance of the money be paid immediately. They felt if he could afford a new car, then we should be able to pay them back in full. And that is exactly what happened. Logically, it made sense and I can understand where they were coming from, but it could have been handled differently. But for "me," there was never a compromise! There could have been a discussion as opposed to a demand. I could have explained that the car was bought "on time" rather than buying the car outright for cash.

Those first five years of our marriage were difficult, and I was happy that there were no children yet. It gave me a chance to really see who I was dealing with, not only with him but also his family. My father, once again, gave me good advice and told me to try to hold off having kids since I was so young. I found this to be an interesting comment and wonder if my dad thought the marriage would not last. My father-in-law was quite verbal, however, telling everyone that there was something wrong with me for not getting pregnant immediately, as it was their family tradition to start a family soon after marriage. My mother also pressured me to have a baby, as she wanted to become a grandmother, telling me how much she loved kids. You could've fooled me. I wasn't sure who was living in the twilight zone, me or my mother. That disclosure was quite incongruent with her actions and it blew me away. Honestly, when I got married, I was not interested in having kids, but four years into the marriage, I changed my mind and got pregnant, and it was the best decision I ever made (unlike my father who told me how he felt about having kids). I was still working in an office during my pregnancy and was thrilled when we decided that I would be a stay-at-home mom. Frankly, I don't know how working moms do it. When I observe my daughter and daughter-in-law working full-time, raising kids, and being involved in all their activities, I become exhausted just thinking about it. I barely had enough energy to care for my children, keep house, and run errands, let alone the possibility of holding a paying job outside the home. I am in awe of women who can manage all of the above. The stress, the frenetic balancing of home, work, kids, activities, and trying to continue a relationship with one's spouse was difficult for me to manage.

Today the burden of child rearing is more frequently shared by both partners. My son and son-in-law are active participants in the process of raising their children. It's hard on both parents to juggle work and raising kids while driving them all over the place. I was fortunate that *all* I had to do was raise the kids, do the wash, cook, clean the house, and drive them to all their activities. I did all the running around that Oscar refused or had no interest in doing. Back then raising kids was very oppressive because women were seen as not being productive members of society. Raising kids was "women's work." What's changed is that men *are* more involved with their kids today than when I was growing up.

My daughter, Bernadette, was born in the spring. It was an easy pregnancy and easy delivery, natural childbirth. My parents and my in-laws came to visit me while I was in the hospital. My in-laws, specifically my father-in-law, was unable to censure his thoughts. All babies look alike when they are born and all babies are beautiful. However, as my in-laws approached the hospital room, I could feel the sterility of the room instantly become infected by the germs that seemed to seep underneath the door. The room that was just sanitized by housekeeping now felt grimy and contaminated by the mere presence of Oscar's parents. Here I lay in my hospital bed with my daughter lying in the bassinet alongside my bed, my firstborn who was so perfect, so pure, so beautiful, and so pink. I momentarily turned to look out of the window of my hospital room. I'm sure I was hallucinating at that moment as I imagined a raven perched on the windowsill, on this unseasonably warm sunny day. Was it a premonition of something ominous soon to take place? I felt my insides, my intestines, which were once organized in a fully functioning fashion, now emotionally entangled, unable to digest whatever was going to happen next. As my in-laws entered the room and gazed down at the bassinet at this sleeping infant, I could see my father-in-law's glaring eyes looking at my daughter with this mysterious, jeering look on his face. I said to myself, "What now?" I was unable to predict what happened next. The only thing, the very first thing, my father-in-law could say was the following: "Thank God she doesn't have nigger lips like her mother." My father-in-law always looked down upon me for being Italian, specifically, part Sicilian. Additionally, there were always innuendos about my lack of education when I was in their presence; however, this was clearly a projection on his part. He was the stupid one for saying such a disgusting thing. It was a racist comment that was meant to hurt and be offensive. It was quite clear how he felt about me. However, I was most upset because Oscar allowed such a foul and terrible statement to be said without holding his father accountable. Oscar never had my back, especially when it came to his family. He allowed his father's rudeness, sneering, and vengefulness to be acceptable and commonplace. Oscar would always make excuses for him saying, "You know how he is. He's probably hung over or had a few before he came. Just let it go, he doesn't mean anything by it." The truth was my father-in-law was unable to admit that such a beautiful baby could have possibly come out of my body.

Once I approached Oscar about his father's comment, he claimed he did not hear it. Selective hearing always came in handy when he was around his family. He always had an excuse for his family's behavior, and he was unable to hold them accountable for their actions. Luckily, my mother always wanted to babysit her first grandchild, and I never had to argue with Oscar about his parents watching the kids. There was only one time when we needed someone to watch my daughter for a few hours. My mother-in-law and father-in-law were not people who I would label "responsible or reliable" people. Oscar insisted they watch her using the argument "My mother raised seven kids, why can't she babysit?" My response was, "I'm familiar with her work, I live with you, I'm not impressed with her parenting skills." In my opinion, she *had* seven kids, she did not *raise* seven kids. My daughter and I survived the few hours when she was at my in-laws, but they never babysat for me again.

Two years and four months later, I gave birth to a son. I had a forty-five-minute labor. I barely made it to the hospital with ten minutes to spare. My doctor was on his way home from a delivery at four o'clock in the morning, only to return to the hospital. I was in the delivery room with the nurse who told me not to push because the doctor was not there. As I could actually feel my son coming out of my body, I called the nurse over, grabbed the collar of her scrubs, and asked how many deliveries had she done prior to me. She said, "Countless," and I said, "Well, get ready for another one 'cause this baby is coming *now*!" And then the doctor they called, who lived across the street from the hospital, came in. With my legs in stirrups, he put his hands between my legs and my son came shooting out. He came so fast that his face was squished, and he was "not so cute." However, within twenty-four hours, he pinked-up and was absolutely beautiful. But stupid me thought he would behave just like my daughter, who slept through the night when she was twenty-eight days old. She got up at 7 a.m.

Diane Harth

for breakfast, took a 10 a.m. morning nap, up at noon for lunch, down again at 2 p.m., up again at 4 p.m., dinner at 5 p.m., and back in bed at 7 p.m. This was her routine. My son was a different story.

My son, Jarret, was born with an inguinal hernia that strangulated when he was four weeks old. I knew something was wrong with him immediately. When we got him home, all he did was cry. This was not normal. I brought him to the pediatrician who was a great diagnostician. He told me he had a hernia and I should *immediately* go to a surgeon, which I did. The surgeon wanted to wait until he was eight weeks old and weighed more. My son weighed eight and a half pounds at birth. I was unaware until after his surgery that my pediatrician told the surgeon that his hernia would strangulate and the necessity for surgery was imminent. My pediatrician told me what to look for if it did strangulate, and then, if that happened, I should get to the hospital immediately. On November 1, 1982, Oscar just happened to come home from work early and he was changing my son's diaper and noticed the hernia had strangulated. As one could expect, my pediatrician was off that night and so was the surgeon. We rushed to the hospital. My neighbor took my daughter until my mother arrived to take Bernadette home with her. When my husband and I arrived at the hospital, it was standing room only. We managed to find a seat and waited to be called. I was too upset to wait, so I turned to my husband and said, "I will get their attention," and did something that I was not proud of but most likely saved my son's life. I squeezed his testicles and he wailed. We immediately got the staff's attention and were called in. They wanted to know when he ate last and how much. Since I was nursing him, I told them how long I nursed. That answer did not sit well with them. They needed ounces and we had no way of knowing how many ounces he had. My husband finally said, "My wife doesn't have a gauge on her breast to indicate how much milk he drank." The next step was to transport my son to the pediatric hospital a few blocks away by ambulance. I literally had to hand him over to a nurse and was not allowed to ride in the ambulance with him. I am still baffled as to why I was not allowed in the ambulance. I had racing thoughts of what if he died on the way to the hospital in the ambulance. All I wanted to do was hold him and take care of him. The few blocks we drove behind the ambulance to get to the pediatric hospital seemed endless; it would have seemed faster to drive through the Lincoln Tunnel during rush hour in a blizzard. I told my husband not to stop at any red lights. That was not hard to do, as it was the middle of the night and hardly anyone was on the roads. When we got to the hospital, they had to call in an entire team of pediatric surgical staff. No one wanted to operate on a four-week-old due to the liability.

The interview started the moment we arrived at the pediatric hospital. They completely stripped him looking for any indication of foul play, bruises, or physical abuse caused by me, to be exact. The nurse said, "Well, I don't see any bruises," looking at me, her face stern and deliberate, as if she seemed disappointed that she couldn't accuse me of beating him. She then decided to check him

Diane Harth

again, questioning me again about my handling of him. I told her that he was scheduled for surgery within the next few weeks and she should check the hospital's records. She continued to question me up and down, just short of saying I abused him with no evidence to support her claim. Finally, the surgeon was on the phone demanding the patient come to the OR.

I am not a religious person, more like a failed Catholic, but it bothered me that he was not yet baptized. I thought, "Why did this happen this week and not next week after he was baptized?" Oscar and I walked up and down the hallways, for what seemed to be hours, thinking the worst but never, *never*, talking about it. He was only four weeks old. Finally, after about two hours, the surgeon came out and told us he was fine. He did mention it was a close call and if we had waited a bit longer, my son probably would not have made it. Everything inside him was screwed up. His intestines were wrapped around his testicles cutting off his blood supply. But he made it through. I slept at the hospital that night. He was in this incubator and the only way I could touch him was through an opening on the sides of the incubator. He was only in the hospital for that night and we brought him home the next morning. I am grateful that he will never remember.

I should have predicted his hernia as my daughter also had hernia surgery when she was a year old. Hers did not strangulate. For decades, whenever I heard ambulance sirens on November 1, I would think of that night, tear up, and be grateful he is still with us.

When Jarret was about six years old, we were at my kids' school for its yearly carnival fundraiser. As I walked around with him, I saw the woman, the nurse who held him in the ambulance. I will never forget her. She was a short woman, a bit on the heavy side, with gray hair and warm smile. I approached her and asked if she remembered this particular incident. She did and was happy to see my son. She said she never forgot that evening and how upset I was when I handed him over to her. She told me this was one of those cases you don't forget.

Diane Harth

Chapter 15

THE LURE OF PLASTIC

Oscar continued to travel a lot for work and I stayed home with the kids. He was gone at least once a month for about a week but that varied. I would go visit my mother so she could help me with the kids and give me a bit of a break, but she said something to me that was crystal clear. "Because of my son's emergency surgery," my mother said, "I'm not watching your kids by myself anymore." The pediatrician said my son may develop an inguinal hernia on his left side. She was fearful of him having to go to the hospital again while in her care.

During my son's first year of life, I hired a babysitter, a high school student who had a very good reputation and was very reliable. She was amazing with the kids and the kids loved her. She enjoyed being around the kids, playing with them, and making sure they were always safe. Over the years, the kids looked forward to being with her and would run up to her the minute she came into the house. She was also one of the few people who could put my son to sleep with little to no problem. She was a godsend. She was so helpful that we even took her on vacation with us once. She lived in the same town, making it very convenient for us to pick her up to babysit. Once or twice a week she would come after school for a couple of hours just so I could get out of the house without the kids. I became less dependent on my mother, which also decreased my anxiety.

But something was missing in my life, in addition to love, companionship, trust, and understanding. I needed normal adult socialization, aside from my dysfunctional family. Several years earlier, I had met June, who lived two blocks away yet separated by a river. June was married to someone Oscar worked with and we would get together once a month on a Friday night for dinner, prior to my kids being born. Little did I know at the time that forty-six years later, she would still be my BFF.

June is about five feet five inches, give or take, attractive and slender with blond hair. She has a great laugh, is warm, and always comforting. Being around June was like putting on an old pair of jeans. *So* comfortable, so soft and relaxing. She always knew the right thing to say at the right time and would put a positive spin on everything. But most importantly, she was trustworthy. She did not gossip, so I knew if she was not talking about other people, she also was not talking about me. What this meant to me was that she was a confidant! I knew whatever I told her would stay with her. I had no awareness when I met her that all of her wonderful qualities were penetrating deep inside my unconsciousness, embedding themselves, lying dormant in my brain, waiting for the right moment to enter my consciousness. I realize, today, decades later after I remarried, I actually married someone with the same qualities and characteristics as June.

Diane Harth

June had a great relationship with her husband. This was my first introduction to what a healthy relationship looked like. They were comfortable with each other and kind to each other. It was so foreign to me. Their relationship resonated with me and eventually became absorbed into my skin, the way the sun beats down on you on a summer day. I always felt the warmth when in their presence. An early hint that I might be in the wrong relationship.

June's neighbor worked as a Tupperware salesperson and tried to recruit me when my son was an infant. At the time, I was very sleep-deprived and not ready to take on another task. But by the time my son was two years old, I was ready to do something for myself. So, I became a Tupperware salesperson.

And then I went into panic mode and my anxiety reached a level that I had not felt since I was a teenager. How do I tell my mother? I was thirty years old and afraid of telling my mother that I was contemplating working outside the home. I know my readers are thinking, how can a thirty-year-old, married for several years with two kids, still be afraid of her mother? The absurdity of just the thought of it.

My maternal grandmother was not doing well at that time as dementia had set in. My aunt was overloaded caring for her, so my mother went to Brooklyn and spent a few days with them to relieve her sister. That gave me some time to think of a way of telling her while limiting the potential of criticism and verbal abuse at the same time. I had childcare covered between my babysitter and Oscar, as Oscar agreed to come home earlier on those nights that the babysitter was unavailable. Because my mother had a great deal of influence over me, I had to prepare ahead of time for an avalanche of negativity. Therefore, I agreed to sell Tupperware and got all the information I needed, setting myself up as a dealer, before telling my mother. I was committed and left myself no room to back out of this commitment.

My mother returned home from Brooklyn. I called her, as her phone only worked one way; incoming calls only. She asked, "What's new?" and, remember, she was not really interested in me and in the allotted time of two minutes before she was able to focus on herself, I told her, "I'm going to be selling Tupperware." In my head, I expected to hear how I would be emotionally damaging my kids for not being there for them at night, to feed them, bathe them, and put them to sleep. They would be emotionally scarred, feeling abandoned and resentful, as children need their mother. Ironic! I wondered how much guilt she would put on me, as I was her target in her emotional dunk tank. I was her psychological object and her focus on me was flawless, which always resulted in her hitting the target and my falling in the water. All she wanted was to emotionally drown me in that dunk tank. She wanted me to be like her and not succeed at anything. Her expectation was that I would not learn how to survive in the water, leaving me dependent on her forever. That's what *she* needed: her own survival depended on her children's dependence on her. Her need to be loved. After all, how could I succeed when she knew she never could? Once again, I was surprised by her response.

Diane Harth

She said to me, "Wow, that's great," and went on about how difficult her week was at her sister's house. I imagine she was more focused on her own mother's decline rather than concentrating on me. As I exhaled, I realized that I had avoided the criticism, which was a rare occurrence.

These mixed messages I received from her were mind-boggling. It was schizophrenic. I never knew if she was going to be the good witch or the bad witch on any given day. But my kids were not emotionally scarred; they felt safe and secure with the sitter and had a healthy attachment to her. I also role-modeled for my kids that women can rely on themselves and do not have to be dependent on just one person for survival. I was beginning to independently organize my life and manage my anxiety.

Little did I know Tupperware would have a major impact on my life! Tupperware gave me a sense of confidence in myself that I never had before. The people who sold this product were positive, very positive, with a message that it's possible to be the best and be successful. I loved the product and was a good salesperson. Within a couple of years, I recruited four women and became a manager. I got a company car, which made Oscar very happy. I was in the top ten of new managers in sales on the East Coast. My self-esteem, for the first time in my life, increased. I felt like Mary Tyler Moore throwing her hat in the air on the streets of Minneapolis. I had my own money, not much, but it was mine. I set up a bank account in my own name. I felt empowered. However, the memories of my first job when I was a teen came back to me. This small bit of independence somehow kicked me in the ass after my first paycheck and I apprehensively waited for that kick to appear. But, again, what was unexpected and simultaneously not surprising was how Oscar refused to pay for certain things now that I had my own money.

Selling Tupperware gave me a sense of validation and competence. The dealers knew me, respected me, and competed against me with regard to being recognized as having achieved the highest weekly sales. I felt important for the first time in my life.

Chapter 16

"IT'S NOT ME, IT'S YOU," SAID OSCAR

When I turned twenty-nine, I had an awakening, a real "aha" moment before I even knew what an "aha" moment actually meant. I woke up one morning and a thought, an insight, came into my head. My unconscious had been at work. Experiences stay in the unconscious because it's too dangerous for these events to become conscious. They only become conscious when your brain knows it can emotionally handle whatever it is that you experienced, that which was originally too devastating. I realized that I did not "like" my mother. I was able to admit to myself that I didn't like the person she was and how she treated me. This was the beginning of a change in my relationship with her. I still wanted her approval but not as much. Simultaneously, I also realized that I was a feminist and was tired of the patriarchy. I don't know how I came to this realization but I did. My mother had lived fulfilling the gender-stereotypical, culturally approved wifely role. Because of this, she had a third child she resented. So, I paid the price of patriarchy. It is likely that working in Tupperware, and having been exposed to so much positivity from these women I was involved with for a few years, enabled me to see myself as a success instead of a failure. It increased my self-esteem. I started to feel better about myself as a person.

This was around the same time when Oscar approached me about couples therapy. What's interesting is that he probably realized that he was no longer the focus of my attention. He said, "We are just cohabitating," which was true. He complained about the lack of intimacy in our marriage. From my perspective, he never defended me to his family, and he complained publicly about our "lack of intimacy," which was humiliating to me. There was no emotional support, love, or kindness. He was a workaholic, was rarely home, spent little time with me, and the only thing he wanted to fix was our sex life—nothing else. If women feel emotionally connected to their partner, intimacy rarely is an issue. But for Oscar, if he was having sex, then the marriage was good. The emotional stuff didn't matter to him at all as long as he was getting what he wanted. Hence, let's go to therapy to fix "her."

He chose the therapist and made the appointment. I have no memory of having any preconceived thoughts about it. I have no memory of being anxious. Maybe in my unconscious I was feeling that, possibly, Oscar will get "fixed" (not necessarily being neutered, because I knew I could, figuratively, do that all on my own). I, honestly, did not know what to expect. But as you will see later on, this was the first of two suggestions he made to me that came back to bite *him* in the ass.

We got to our first appointment. The therapist's office was about ten minutes away from our house. We walked up a dimly lit staircase into a fairly small waiting room. As we entered there was a tiny reception area on the left side where we checked in and paid the fee. We sat down and to the right was a bathroom. I must have been a bit anxious, as I have no recollection if there were any pictures on the wall. There were about three or four treatment rooms, all different sizes, some small, some large. A man approached the waiting room and called us by name. He was not much taller than me, maybe five eight, five nine, dark hair with a beard and mustache. We followed him into one of the smaller rooms and sat down. He took down an extensive family history. I said to myself, "Great, maybe he will see what I see and Dr. D will understand why I can't be close to Oscar."

Since this happened over forty years ago my memory is not very clear as to who started talking first about their family history. I am not sure if Oscar described his family first, or if I did, but we spent a couple of weeks on our biological families. I believe it was the third or fourth session when he wanted us to come in separately. I remember having the individual session first. Never being in therapy before, I had no idea about confidentiality and that the therapist was forbidden to divulge anything to anybody. As I look back on those sessions, it is hard for me to comprehend how Dr. D was able to deal with me. I was unable to trust that he would be a confidant. After all, if I could not trust my mother and I could not trust my husband, how could

I trust a total stranger? Dr. D had the patience of a saint. I stayed with him for three years. Three years in individual therapy. With my first individual session, Dr. D explored the relationship between me and my parents, particularly my mother. I will assume that he did the same with Oscar because it was shortly after Oscar had his first individual session that he dropped out of treatment. Oscar was not capable of saying anything negative about his family, especially his mother. He was not capable of being objective about them either. A therapist would only have an accurate history of his family if he continued with treatment for a much longer time.

The reason why I say Dr. D had the patience of a saint, was because I had the same answer for every question he asked, "I don't know." I was never able to trust anyone, so how could I possibly trust him? At one point he gave me a test to take home, possibly a personality test. I took the test and a few weeks later he said one thing. The test showed that I had no trust in anything! That didn't surprise me.

Dr. D, however, was surprised. He worked with me, and after about two years, I started to come around. I started talking to him and disclosing my feelings. I started to trust him. I realized this was the only place, aside from Tupperware, where I was getting attention. Positive attention. Attention with no criticism and total validation. It was my safe place. One day, he asked me something very interesting. It was probably the most consequential session I have ever had. As he sat in his chair a few feet away from the couch I was sitting on, he had a look of intent. There was a seriousness about him that I never saw previously. His face was solemn, sedate. His eyes were fixed and he was not blinking. As he glanced in my direction and looked directly into my eyes, he asked me a series of questions. He asked: "Did you ever do any drugs, drop some acid, smoke pot, anything at all? Were you ever arrested? Did you ever steal anything? Did you have lots of sex with lots of guys? What was the worst thing you ever did?" I looked at him, confused as to why he was asking me these questions. I focused on his face and said, "I would come home two minutes late past my curfew." He asked, "That's it, no drugs, no sex, no arrests?" I said, "No." He looked at me in a way I had never seen before. That flat affect that most clients see on their therapists' faces, no expression, seemed to leave him. I saw a look that I can only describe as being puzzled and a look of empathy, both at the same time. His eyes softened, the glare of confusion had left him. His posture changed from being stiff and upright to a more relaxed position. In retrospect, I can assume that my answer did not fit into his working hypothesis. After a few minutes of metabolizing what I had said—and when a therapist is silent, seconds, minutes, feel like hours—he turned to me and said: "You are not the problem, you've done nothing wrong. It sounds like you were a really good kid." In my head, his words hit me like a lightning bolt that can be seen on the ocean, on the horizon, that precedes the crack of thunder. What, me, a good kid? Maybe he's delusional, I thought. That was the first time someone acknowledged me for who I really was. I realized at that point that I needed someone to recognize that I was an innocent bystander and a scapegoat for my family. Of course, I was a "bystander." After all, at Radio City I actually became a bystander. I was the product of parents who were not emotionally equipped to raise a "typical teenager." I also realized, on a more conscious level, that Oscar blamed me for his unhappiness, and he had hoped therapy would change me, make me more submissive to him. Both Mom and Oscar blamed me. They projected their own unhappiness onto me. Therapy did change me but not in a way that he wanted or would have been satisfied with.

In that last year of therapy with Dr. D, I made great progress. Once again, I had another "aha" moment. One day I realized that for the first time in my life I actually "liked myself." It was shocking to hear myself say that, mainly because I never realized that I did not like myself. It was amazing. I remember calling Dr. D and telling him this. This "aha" moment changed my life. It was a game-changer, and I have Dr. D to thank for that. It was also a point in my life when I realized my marriage was dead, but it would be years before I could extract myself from this relationship.

Therapy is not a one-way street. Therapy takes time, not just a few sessions and you're fixed. Dr. D had the patience and the compassion to work with me. But I also had the drive and desire to want to change myself. Therapy does not work if the client does not want to do the work. Therapy is about allowing yourself to be vulnerable with the therapist. It takes lots of time. For thirty years, I was behaving in a way that was not healthy, and like most people, I internalized what my parents told me. It takes years to deconstruct and reconstruct behavior. People present to the world a camouflaged image of themselves in order to protect themselves from external and internal attacks, which serves as a defensive trench in which they are trapped. Periodically, they may peer out of the trench and retreat into the "safety of that trench." This peering out is their barometric evaluation to determine whether "all is quiet on the western front."

Chapter 17

THE ROAD TO INDEPENDENCE

After about three years in treatment, I terminated my sessions with Dr. D. I felt I was in a good place. I also felt my perception had shifted to a more positive outlook instead of a negative outlook. The combination of therapy and my Tupperware family enabled me to believe in myself. My coping skills were healthier and more appropriate than my dysfunctional ways of dealing with the world previous to treatment. Once someone decides to discontinue treatment and feels more independent and less dependent on the therapist, that's when you know the treatment has worked. However, people stay in treatment for many years for many different reasons. The other reason was that I was paying for my own therapy. Once I started working again, Oscar refused to pay for the treatment. I was not making a lot of money and it felt quite punitive. He was behaving like my mother. He said to me, "It builds character." And that was the "kick in the ass."

I also stopped selling Tupperware around the same time. I was burned out, and I no longer needed to prove to myself that I could be successful and accomplished. This sense of accomplishment was a surprise to me, as I had always felt insecure and inadequate. My sales were always high, and I was working about four parties a week. I was tired and started to lose interest in the job. But I still wanted to work. I got a job working at a doctor's office as a receptionist, just for the extra money and to get out of the house. But that job was not fulfilling. It was just that, a job. I needed something more. I talked to Oscar about how I was feeling. Little did he know this "second suggestion," the first suggestion being couples' therapy, would change both of our lives forever; mine in a positive way, his in a negative way. But Oscar was always self-serving. Any suggestions he would make to me were more about how it would make him look and not about how it would benefit me. As we stood in the kitchen, me expecting little from this conversation and him expressionless, I waited for what he was going to say. The words that came out of his mouth were something unanticipated. He suggested that I go to college. What my husband never realized was that I was aware of what he was actually saying. That cartoon bubble, the speech balloon, appeared above his head telling me exactly what he thought. What he was actually saying was "Take a few courses to keep yourself occupied." His intention was not for me to get a degree but to basically just focus on something else besides complaining to him about how much time he spends at work. What he was really saying was "Do something with your life so you won't bother me." He was tired of hearing me complain about him being a workaholic. He really had no interest in what I was doing. He had an ulterior motive. I learned over the years that Oscar's primary goal in life was Oscar.

He was unable to do anything that would not benefit him, which contradicted what he constantly said to me: "My goal in life is to make you happy." Happiness comes from within yourself. Happiness is a feeling you have deep inside of you. He was not capable of loving me and I needed to be loved. Therefore, his goal of making me happy could never be achieved, and as long as I was with him, my goal of being loved could never be achieved either.

If we look at this from the other way around, what would make Oscar happy? For the marriage to be happy for Oscar, it needed to be all about him. This was a trigger for me; he was behaving like my mother. Oscar's happiness would come from having more intimacy. I was unable to provide this to him because he was emotionally distant. The unhappiness was a two-way street.

I thought about his "suggestion." I knew exactly what I wanted to do with my life. I wanted to be a therapist and have my own practice. Be my own boss. I did not want to work for anyone. I believe I was emotionally incapable of answering to an authority figure because I would feel controlled. I felt if "this hot mess" could change her own behavior, her own thought process, if she was able to have positive feelings about herself after a life of hating herself by just talking to someone, then maybe, just maybe, she could have the potential of helping others. There must be something to this. I wasn't looking to make tons of money; that wasn't me, that was all Oscar. I was looking for a career that I would enjoy, that I would love, a career that would make me feel I've made a difference in the world. But the most important thing was that I believed in the process of therapy.

However, my unconscious was, again working overtime; there was another motive. If I could get my degree, I would be able to work at a job that was substantial and respectable and would enable me to get out of this marriage. I could, hopefully, be financially independent. But this thought did not surface into my awareness for a couple of years. It emerged into my consciousness like a snake slowly slithering around, the way it sneaks up on its prey in the woods, waiting to catch it by surprise. And this unconscious thought only became conscious years later.

Originally, I was set on going to William Paterson College. There is no reason as to why I decided on Willie P. I thought it was the place to be and decided to apply. I sent in my application and essay. I received information in the mail regarding registering for courses, but the correspondence I received was vague. I tried to speak to someone at the registrar's office to no avail. Admissions seemed to be disorganized, and for some reason registering for classes was a monumental task. I was never able to get a straight answer from them about anything. I was still working for the doctor and discussed this with him. I said to him, "I don't think this is going to work out at all." He said, "Don't give up, forget Willie P, apply to Ramapo, it's a very good college." And I took his advice.

I did my research and saw that registration for the spring semester closed on Friday. That was three days away. I immediately got on the bat phone and called June. I said,

"I'm going to register for college on Friday, wanna come?" June said, "I don't think I'm doing anything on Friday, sure, why not." And Friday came, we got in the Batmobile with our capes fluttering in the wind, and drove to Ramapo College and registered for courses. I'm not sure if June knew what she wanted to major in; however, I knew exactly what I wanted to do, major in psychology.

The college was only about twenty minutes away from our houses. Having never been on a college campus before, I did not know what to expect. We arrived at the parking lot, which seemed huge, primarily because it was unfamiliar. We parked the car and started trudging up what seemed to be a long, steep hill, thinking "Thank God, hills only go in one direction; leaving will be easier."

Luckily, it was a very small campus. The people were friendly enough to direct us to the registrar's office. This was the last day of registration and the realization of classes being filled up and being told "this class is closed" was contradictive to what I had in mind.

June and I decided to take classes together, at least to start with. We decided to take Intro to Psychology. As I approached the desk to register, I said with such confidence, "Just put me in Intro to Psychology." The registrar said, "It's completely full and I can't allow anyone else in." I said to myself, "What do you mean there's no more room, this is the course I want." It was at this point I truly understood the phrase "The early bird gets the worm." I was not taking no for an answer. I boldly and with some arrogance said, "Who can I talk to about this?"

It was suggested to us that we go to the psych department and see if they would sign us both into the class. In the meantime, we decided to register for any course just to start and then take it from there. So, we went to the psych department and spoke to the person who would be able to get us signed into the class. We lucked out and both of us were signed into the class. On some level, this reinforced my rebellious nature of not taking "no" for an answer and to keep pushing until I got what I wanted. But I've always been smart enough to know when to push the envelope and when to keep my mouth shut.

We were both very happy. This was the start of our college careers. We carpooled to school for the first few semesters when we had the same classes. June eventually decided to major in social work, and I remained in psychology, in the School of Theoretical and Applied Science.

But college was tough for me because it reminded me of my elementary and high school years. Academically, I struggled, and my grades were nothing to brag about. I did not have the kind of book smarts that June had. I had to work very hard to get good grades. Reading was not my strong suit (remember first grade) as I didn't comprehend well. I read and read and reread my psych book until I understood the message the author was trying to convey. I spent hours during the day while my kids were at school trying to understand theory. I did very well in that class and all my hard work paid off.

I believe the last class June and I took together was biology. During that class, I became aware of an interesting phenomenon. It does not matter how old you are when you're in school, there will always be mean girls. June and I always sat next to each other. There were maybe two or three other returning students in the class, and for some reason, they did not like us. There were always snide comments coming from them aimed toward us such as "What, no tennis lesson today?" I believe they thought we were "privileged." We just ignored them. We did get the last laugh though. If you had an A average in the class, you would be exempt from the final exam. And June and I were exempt, the only ones exempt—and the professor announced it in the class. We did not react to this announcement, however, once the class was over and we left, we high-fived and laughed all the way home. But, again, this class was difficult for me to grasp, to the point of approaching the professor and telling him I couldn't understand the text. He gave me another book, an older edition of the same book that was easier to understand. That's how I passed biology.

It took us six years to get through college. We took summer classes, and as time went on increased our course load. But college continued to be a struggle for me. Nothing came easy, and I continued to work hard and be disciplined.

A math class was required in order to graduate from college. Algebra to be exact. I had not taken any advanced math in high school, so to me, algebra was like taking a foreign language. I had to take a remedial class in algebra and hired a private tutor, whom I met when I was selling Tupperware. She was able to teach me in a way that I could understand. Lucky for me, the state rules had changed months before I took the course, otherwise I would still be in college. Previously, you had to pass the state exam in order to pass the class. Passing the class and failing the state exam would not allow you to obtain the credits for the course. They changed the requirements, which stated you could fail the state exam as long as you passed the algebra class. For two semesters, whenever I closed my eyes, all I saw were numbers and letters on the inside of my eyelids. Numbers and letters should never go together. God made Adam and Eve, but I refuse to believe that he or she intended for numbers and letters to be an item. It was too confusing for me. Algebra was the most tedious, mind-boggling class I ever took. It was brutal. I was unable to grasp it. I told my professor that so far, I had gotten through life without it, and I would continue to get through life without it when this class was over. As far as I was concerned, it was not useful to me. It was anxiety-provoking. It's been said that algebra helps you think critically. It is hard for me to believe algebra helped me to analyze my clients. It is hard to believe algebra played a part in how I evaluated my clients, my work, or myself, and I was able to be a therapist without the use of the combination of numbers and letters. The reason I became a therapist was because there was no math involved.

However, one day a couple came into my office, sat down, and said they had a math problem they wanted me to solve. I said to myself, "Holy shit, they didn't teach me this is social work school." I started to break out into a cold sweat. My muscles tightened and I felt panicked. Then I thought, I just need to come clean and tell them math is not my strong suit. So, first, I listened to what the problem was, and it was more of a common-sense issue than a math problem. I don't remember the details of the problem, but it was about buying tickets for a show. Thank God it was not a word problem like "If we leave our house at five o'clock traveling sixty miles an hour and our friends who live further away leave at four o'clock traveling fifty miles an hour, and the other couple live closer traveling fifty-five miles an hour, who would get there first?" That is where I would have drawn the line. I might have even said, "Free session if you never bring in another math problem again." I debated putting a sign on my door saying, "I can handle all problems except math problems." But I did neither. I survived algebra with the help of my tutor. I got an A- in the class and I never used algebra again. As an aside, I did, in fact, flunk the state exam; however, as I said previously, it didn't matter at all.

Once I really got into my major and was taking mostly psychology classes, that's when I really started to come into my own. Ramapo was very liberal. The professors were great, and I experienced something new to me. The support that I was exposed to in Tupperware was what I also found in college. The professors took an interest in their students. There was guidance, direction, and support from the faculty that enabled me to grow as a person. The positiveness, the feeling that one can be anything they wanted to be, was palpable. I became much more of an independent thinker than I had ever been.

There were three psychology professors who had a major impact on my life. I learned about what it meant to be a feminist and had a better understanding about the oppression of women from the classes I took with them. I learned that being a feminist doesn't mean women hate men. It means equal rights for *all* people, not just women. I learned about patriarchy and gained a better understanding of my family. It was at that time that I decided to minor in women's studies. It was a real eye-opener, and I flourished even more.

I took a course in feminist epistemology. At the time, I had no idea what the heck "epistemology" meant and took the course because it dealt with being a feminist. By the way, epistemology means "a way of knowing, theory of knowledge." I took this course with one of my three favorite professors. His teaching style was impressive and "not boring." One day, he told us he was going to divide the class into two groups and do an experiment. The experiment was called BaFa BaFa. One group was run by an authoritarian leader and the other was democratic and egalitarian. The class was not informed about how these groups were going to be handled. However, no surprise to me, I got stuck in the authoritarian group but was unaware, like everyone else, how this would play out. I should have just stayed home, as I have been in this experiment for a lifetime. The professor was the leader of the authoritarian group and "he" ordered everyone around. You had to listen to what "he" said, no questions asked. This was a very big trigger for me. So, I decided I wasn't going to play. Yup, I told the professor I was done. I sat in the back of the room and like a little kid folded my arms and watched the other students behaving like puppets, taking orders from the professor, feeling as if they had nothing to say. I was not concerned about the consequences. I did not care if this negatively affected my grade, as it could not have been any worse than what I had experienced growing up. My rebellious nature reared its ugly head again!

After the experiment was done, we all sat with our desks in a circle in the classroom and processed what had transpired. The class was enraged by my behavior. Upset that I had protested, they asked, "How could you do this?" Interestingly, I had the same thought about them—"How could they do this, just listen with no objection?" But I did not care! Surprisingly, and much to the class's amazement, this is just what the professor wanted. He wanted someone to protest. He said in the twenty years of doing this experiment, no one ever protested. I was the first, and this was the entire purpose of the experiment, to protest the patriarchy.

Some of the students in the class hated me. Not sure why, maybe because I was recognized for what I did in that experiment. But I was not interested in accolades or to kiss ass. This experiment was way too uncomfortable for me. Later on in the semester, I found out from other students in the class that these students wanted to slash my tires and were planning on waiting for me in the parking lot. They really didn't scare me. After all, it was not high school anymore! These students never said anything to my face, never confronted me, so it really didn't affect me too much. If they were really serious, they would have threatened me in some way and wouldn't have just talked about me behind my back. So, I just ignored the rumors.

Being a returning student and married with children, bullies didn't mean much to me. Besides, they were unskilled and inexperienced at bullying, and based on what I experienced in my life, between my family and in-laws, they were small potatoes. Surprisingly, on the last day of the semester, they approached me and apologized to me. Why they apologized is still a mystery to me. But here is a spoiler alert. Years later, this professor married me.

By the time I was a junior in college, I realized that graduate school was a necessity in order for me to become a therapist. Sometimes, ignorance is bliss, and having all the information beforehand might have dissuaded me from pursuing my dream, primarily due to the lack of confidence I had in myself. It might have been too daunting at the time. I spoke to several professors about how to proceed. I wanted to be a psychologist. However, I had to take the Graduate Record Examinations, and getting into a clinical psych program was tough and acceptance was limited to a few students a year. I was just as good at standardized tests as I was at algebra. My other option was to get a Master's degree in Social Work. The GREs were not a requirement to get into a master's of social work (MSW) program. That is when I decided to become a social worker. It might have been the easy way out, but it was also the cheaper way out and only three more years of school. Besides, the only difference between a psychologist and social worker is the training. Both professions do the same thing with respect to private practice.

Chapter 18

ENLIGHTENMENT

Near the end of my college career, I talked to professors about working with battered women. I am sure my personal experience of neglect from both my family of origin and my marriage had something to do with my decision. One of my professors suggested I do an internship at a battered women's shelter. He said it is better to find out what you like and do not like, what you can handle and cannot handle, before you go any further. He said it is safer to experiment with certain populations while you are in school than wait until you're out of school. June knew someone who worked at a shelter and put me in touch with her to at least figure out how to contact the shelter.

I started out doing an internship at a shelter that was about forty-five minutes from my house. It was way out in the country. There was no comparison to the neighborhood I lived in in Pompton Lakes, which I always considered to be the "country." The internship took place in its general office. I would sit in on group therapy and would help with the children's group. I was eventually hired to work at the actual shelter. That location was even further out in the country, real farmland, with few street signs. It was basically, when you come to the cows, make a left turn.

I continued to work at the shelter after I graduated from college and was in my first year of grad school. I had to take a six-week course in domestic violence before I was allowed in the actual shelter. But this experience was the real deal. I realized I had lived a privileged life compared to the women at the shelter. My life did not compare to what these women experienced. I never had to escape from my home due to a threat by my partner trying to kill me by setting the house on fire or by trying to stab me with a knife. I was never locked in my house with no way out. I never experienced physical abuse; for me, it was just neglect. I learned from these women—and I learned a lot. The women in the shelter taught me and gave me strength I never knew I had. The women who passed through the shelter all said the same thing. The emotional abuse is worse than the physical abuse. The bruises go away and the bones heal, but the emotional abuse stays with you forever. And that is an understatement.

These women also did not have the financial advantages that I had. Oscar and I were married for about twenty years when I worked at the shelter. I knew for a long time that I had to leave him, but I was terrified. Oscar always told me, since the time the kids were born, that if I ever left him, *he* would get custody of the kids because he had all the money and power. I was too stupid to know any different, and I was not going to let that happen. This was one of the main reasons why I stayed as long as I did. But now I was educated and knew how to obtain information. The shelter empowered me. Walking away from him would also mean walking away from my mother, as they were one and the same.

I had many more advantages than the women in the shelter, but at the time these women had so much more emotional strength than I did. Yes, they were running for their lives, I wasn't. Most, not all, were uneducated. Some had no families to depend on, no jobs, no money. But domestic violence does not discriminate. It can happen to anyone.

I learned a great deal working in the shelter. I worked an overnight shift. I was able to take a short nap but was awake most of the time due to having to answer the hotline. This taught me a great deal. I learned how to tune into voice quality, pauses, and tone, which became essential for my future career as a therapist. The pauses in someone's voice were fascinating. Why was someone pausing? What emotion were they feeling: guilt, shame, embarrassment? It was educational. It was not possible to observe nonverbal communication on the hotline; therefore, my sixth sense had to come into play.

I worked there for a couple of years and left. The pay was minimum wage, it was a long commute, and my boss despised me and refused to give me a raise. She told me I triggered her but didn't explain why. I have no idea how I triggered her, as I was not even aware that I was doing that until she told me. However, this was something *she* had to work on and come to grips with, not me, since I had no idea what the issue was with me. So, I quit.

Diane Harth

This working experience was worth the commute, the minimum wage, and my difficult boss. The exposure to this population was not only beneficial to my career but also to my personal life and my own decision to leave the marriage. It empowered me!

Chapter 19

GRADUATION

I never thought, anticipated, or expected that I would ever graduate from college. Given my past, there were very low expectations for me, even those I put on myself. But there I was, middle-aged and a senior in college. June had finished her courses in December, and I finished mine in May. I had to figure out where I was going to go to grad school because New York City was not an option. Both Fordham and NYU had MSW classes on campuses outside the city. Outside the city was perfect for me. I applied to both schools. What I was unaware of was that NYU required interviews in the city. I was not happy about that. It was a group interview, and I was unsure of how I was going to get into the city without depending on Oscar. Unfortunately, I had to depend on him to drive me in. I knew he would be unhappy about it, but he took me in. He waited for me outside the conference room, took me home when the interview was over, and then he went to work.

I was told by some of the students I knew at Ramapo that when I go to the interview, I should stay clear of presenting myself as a feminist because they said NYU frowns on feminists. You can only guess what I did. They asked me questions based on my essay, which was oriented toward being a feminist. There were about twenty students in this group interview. I was the only one that was waitlisted. I know that because when I did not hear from the school during the period of time that I should have heard, I called and spoke to the person who had conducted the interview. He told me I was the only one who was waitlisted. I thought it was a bit harsh. Obviously, feminists need not apply!

The evening of the interview, Oscar came home late from work. The moment he walked through the door, he was upset with me because he had had to go into work late after driving me into the city. He was pissed. I wasn't surprised. He said he had a bad day, lots of work he wasn't able to get to, and told me it was my fault that he had to drive me into NY that day. I simply turned to him and said, "If you had to do something for your mother, you never would've complained, but because it was for me, you take issue with it." The conversation went no further.

I waited to hear from Fordham. It was agonizing. I had never felt stress like this before. There was enormous pressure resting on my shoulders. It was like being at the gym for the very first time. My trainer was demonstrating how to do an exercise with ten-pound weights, one in each hand. He told me to raise my arms above my head and bring my arms down again, for twelve reps. I was thinking, this is a piece of cake. As I raised my arms above my head, he stopped me and said, "Don't forget, you must use the weights." Now, ten-pound weights do not sound like a great deal of weight, but when you're exercising for the first time in your life, you actually feel like you're bench-pressing a freaking elephant.

I could not escape these feelings of possibly not getting into grad school. It was all I thought about for days, weeks. The perseverating, the obsessive thoughts; "What if I don't get in, I will never be able to fulfill my dream." All of this would have been a waste, and I would never be able to leave Oscar. I couldn't sleep. The images of depending on Oscar forever were with me when I woke up in the morning until I went to sleep at night. The level of anxiety was enormous, monumental, and unbearable. I tried to distract myself and keep busy, but it was more than I could handle. These emotions wouldn't subside until I knew I was accepted. But like always, I had a backup plan. I could go as a non-matriculating student to start, and, provided my grades were acceptable, I could eventually be accepted into the program.

I finally decided to call the school to see when it would be sending out the letters. The person who answered the phone told me that I should be hearing "good news" very shortly, and days later I received my acceptance letter in the mail. I was finally able to exhale.

Once I received my acceptance package, Oscar told me that I was now on my own (déjà vu, another kick in the ass), and he was not going to pay for graduate school. I reminded him that I paid for his master's degree, and he insisted that he paid for his master's on his own without my help. I did not pursue the conversation because I knew, in the end, it really did not matter. My dream was coming true.

I was in my last semester of college. I was voted the top psych student in my class, and June was the top social work student in her class. There was an award ceremony and I received one thousand dollars toward graduate school. This would come in handy since I was "now on my own." Oscar came to the ceremony. After the ceremony, as we were walking down the hill to the parking lot, he turned to me and said, "I guess it pays to kiss the professor's ass." My first thought, after feeling like I had to vomit, was how can I commit the perfect homicide. I graduated with honors; 3.8 GPA. I did not kiss anyone's ass, and if he was paying any attention to me at all, which he was not, he would have noticed how much time I spent doing homework. I worked very hard for the grades I got. Bastard! But once again, he, all on his own, validated my reasons for divorcing him.

As graduation day grew closer, Oscar kept asking me what I wanted for my graduation. I did not have the heart to tell him I wanted a divorce, so I told him I did not want anything. And that was the truth, I wanted nothing from him. But he kept at it, continuing to ask me what he could get me. I finally said, get me a Walkman just to get him to stop, not realizing this was quite a pun. What I was saying was I wanted to walk away from this man. My unconscious was obviously at work here.

Graduation day came. My parents were there, Oscar, and the kids. Another new chapter. I was with all the graduates getting prepared for the long walk, while my family took their seats, awaiting the graduates to parade down the aisle. Something neither June nor I were aware of was the School of Social Work graduated right before the School of Theoretical and Applied Science. I said to June, be the last person in line from your school and I will be the first person in line from my school to graduate so we can graduate together. And that was what we did.

Chapter 20

OSCAR'S KICK IN THE ASS

I was still in therapy when I started grad school but with a different therapist. Dr. H was recommended to me by one of my favorite psych professors in undergrad. It was a few years since I terminated my treatment with Dr. D. My marriage was not in good shape, and I needed someone to just vent to. I needed someone to help me process my feelings about divorcing Oscar, someone to help "me" and help me to help my kids through this painful experience. My marriage was primarily an extension of my mother's control of me. I no longer loved him. He hurt me to such an extent that I felt I couldn't ever recover if I continued to live with him.

My parents were well aware of our problems and that there was trouble in paradise—the paradise that really never existed, and if this was paradise, I should survive very well in hell. I gave my parents information about the relationship when situations happened like the news ticker, the crawl that one sees on the news at the bottom of the TV screen, mainly because it would have been too much of a shock to them when I filed for divorce. I did not want it to be like putting out the trash on "bulk item disposal day," as this was major furniture that I was putting on the curb. I needed to spread out the amount of criticism that would be thrown at me. My mother would be like a fighter jet strafing the enemy below. I knew I could manage their negativity in small doses. My priority was to take care of my own mental health. That was essential. I knew I would not have my family's support.

I started grad school on the same day my kids had their first day of school. Oscar had told me during the day that we would go out for dinner at the Macaroni Grill since it was the first day of school for everyone.

I was excited about my first day of graduate school. I did not expect my kids to ask me how my day was, as they had other things on their minds about their first day of school. But I guess I overestimated Oscar. We went out to dinner. I decided not to say anything about my day until I was asked. We arrived at the restaurant and waited to be seated. Since it was during the week, it wasn't too long of a wait. There was not too much conversation during the wait to be seated. Bernadette went through the day's events in her class and Jarret talked about what to order and the food on the menu. Food was always on his mind. We eventually got seated. The bread arrived and we were like vultures swarming, hovering over the bread, as if we had never seen or tasted bread before. Their hot bread was absolutely delicious. We ordered our appetizers and our main courses. Oscar asked the kids how their first day of school went and what they learned on their first day. My son told Oscar, "I didn't learn much, I have to go back tomorrow." Our food came and the conversation was really nothing of substance. During the entire meal, Oscar never asked me about my first day of grad school. It was not until the bill arrived that he asked me. By this time, I was annoyed, fuming, my nostrils were flaring. At that point, I felt like a lion. I wanted to slowly move toward my prey, as I contemplated when I should leap upon his back and go for his jugular, when I should break his windpipe, watch him fall, and surrender to my attack. I knew that day would come, but that day was not today. I felt the heat rise within my body, my face turning red and frowning, such that my face was completely contorted and my lips pursed. One would have to be stupid not to realize how upset I was. Why bother asking me now, I thought. My urge was to grab a knife from the table and just fling it toward his eyes, but there was only a butter knife on the table. Once again, I was validated; I had to divorce him. I just sat there and said, "It was fine." I did not go into any detail. At that point, he did not deserve to have any details about what my day was like.

I discussed with Dr. H the general process of going through a divorce, and I knew he had personal experience with this. He gave me the name of a divorce attorney. I did not want someone who was a shark, as my goal was to just get a divorce and not rake him over the coals. I just wanted someone who was fair. I just wanted to be free. I just wanted to be me.

I called the attorney and set up an appointment. I asked June if she would come with me, as I was a bundle of anxiety and needed an additional pair of ears and someone to take notes. June never failed me. I knew I could trust her. I knew my secret would be safe with her. Just meeting with an attorney, just the thought of it, made me shiver. I needed the support of someone who would not judge me, and June never judged me. She was so trustworthy.

So off we went to the attorney's office. I told the attorney that June was only there for that consultation, to take notes and for support. We found out that since I was married for twenty years, I would be entitled to half of everything and since the kids were fourteen and sixteen when we started the process, they were old enough to decide who they wanted to live with. A legal separation in New Jersey does not exist and family court is always backed up; therefore, it would take a few years to finalize. The hard part was going to be that we would have to live in the same house until it was over.

After speaking to the attorney, we sat in the car for a few minutes for me to regain my composure. I was drained, I had no energy, but I was OK. June glanced over at me with her empathic eyes and asked if I was OK. For a moment I thought, can I clone her into a man? I was consumed by my thoughts of how to tell Oscar I was done, that I no longer loved him, that I could no longer live with him. Even more troubling was how to tell the kids.

Grad school was a distraction and I found it to be easy. Ramapo prepared me well for Fordham. Most of what was being taught was something I had already learned. I connected with the students there. Some were traditional ages and some were my age. I felt very comfortable as we were all training to be social workers and were all like-minded.

We traded war stories about our own relationships, and we found comfort in each other. We studied together, collaborated with each other, and helped each other get through difficult concepts that were presented in class.

All of this was good, but I was still consumed with telling Oscar I wanted to leave him. I was unable to get up the courage, I was unsure of how he would react. He was not a violent person. That was not a concern of mine. Even though my attorney said I would be OK financially, there was still a concern about money in my head. Money was the other woman in his life, and, like everyone else who has gone through a divorce, no one ever knows how their spouse will react. I had decided that, financially, if things got really bad, I would live off tuna fish for the rest of my life, and I despise tuna fish, rather than stay in the marriage, or ask my parents for help.

In retrospect, my father prepared me for this change in my life. He always taught me the meaning of a dollar and how to save money. He would say: "When you get a raise at work, you should continue to live like you did prior to the raise. Put that extra money in the bank." Oscar made a very good living, but he didn't spend money. I had no issue with scrimping. I knew how to save money and I knew how to do without.

During the first semester at Fordham, I decided when I would tell him it was over. I could not wait any longer. I had to rip the Band-Aid off, or maybe I should say it was more like a bikini waxing than a Band-Aid. I fantasized how this would go and could not imagine where the screaming was coming from, thinking it was Oscar hearing the news, but the screaming that was going on was in my own head. The conflict that occurred in my head about when to tell him and how to tell him was like two monkeys fighting over one banana. I knew I would be on my own. I knew my parents would not emotionally support me, and I was never going to ask them for financial support.

I remember the evening quite vividly. I had to do this immediately, otherwise, I would lose my courage. He came into the house. The kids were watching TV in the family room. He hung his coat up in the closet in the living room, then hung up his car keys on the key rack in the hallway, which led to the bedroom. He entered the bedroom. I followed him as he walked over to his dresser to put his wallet and change in an ashtray on the shelf on his dresser. And I just blurted it out. I said, "I need to talk to you," and without taking a breath or giving him a chance to say a word, I continued. "I want a divorce by the time I finish grad school." He just looked at me and said nothing. Silence! The silence was deafening, it was like being in the Vatican, but at least in the Vatican you hear a voice, a very loud voice saying, "Silenzio." I walked out of the room. This was the most difficult thing I have ever done in my life and the most courageous thing I have ever done. His silence was oddly strange and confusing to me. One would think when a wife tells her husband she wants a divorce, some sort of conversation would occur. There was no conversation after I said that.

About a week later, my attorney sent him a letter stating that I had retained her and suggested that he retain an attorney. For some reason, when I saw he received the letter, I was not anxious. I remember the look of shock and fear on his face when he saw the envelope. He looked confused. He opened the letter and did not say a word, he even refused to look at me. But later on, after the kids went to bed, we spoke.

He said: "I thought this wasn't going to happen for a few years. I didn't think you were serious." What he was really saying was that he had no idea I had the courage to leave him. After all, in his head he was quite the catch. Oscar never took me seriously, as he always knew he could change my opinion to see things his way. This was the first bold thing I did in the marriage that would negatively affect him.

But then I had to tell my parents I filed for divorce. They did not like this. It was OK for my sister to get a divorce because Dominic orchestrated that divorce. But for me, this wasn't OK. They were most likely afraid I would return to their house and they would have to take care of not only me but my kids. My mother said, "I'll have Dad talk to him and maybe he will get Oscar to change your mind about the divorce." I said: "Mom, I don't want to stay with him, I want the divorce. I can't live like this anymore. Stay out of it, you can no longer control my decisions anymore." She couldn't possibly think that I would leave him, because he was a saint in her eyes, and there was always something wrong with me. I assumed that she thought if we got divorced, it would be Oscar leaving, not me. I am not sure who took the news worse, Oscar or my parents.

One Saturday afternoon, both kids were out of the house. My memory is vague of how Oscar and I got into a screaming match, but I remember we were in the kitchen. He did not want the divorce for two reasons: money and religion. He said to me, "The only reason you are divorcing me is for my money." All of a sudden, the clowns and circus animals were laughing in my head. This was a great line for a standup comedian. I said to him: "If I wanted your money, I would stay married to you. Divorcing you doesn't give me access to your money." And then I said to myself *your money*, I believe the state sees it as equal, not just yours.

He was unable to comprehend what went wrong in the marriage. For the last time, I went down the list. "Your family, there's no love in the marriage, and I am not talking about sex, I mean love. Sex is not love. You never tell me you love me. You don't even like me. I do everything around here with no help from you. All you do is work. I'm not happy living with you." Then there was silence. Then in a very low whisper, in a voice that could only be heard in the quietness of a church confessional, can only be heard in the solemness of one's own head, he said, "I guess I really screwed up." In the twenty years we were together, it was the only time he ever admitted he was wrong and didn't rationalize his behavior. That was the end of our conversation.

Our divorce was, as far as divorces go, described by my attorney as "the poster child of divorces." We lived together with not too much arguing and were able to financially work out the fine details. But it took a long time. Oscar never signed the original document stating I wanted a divorce. This was supposed to be signed within forty-five days of receiving it. It was now over two years. I called him while he was on a business trip. I said to him: "You are in default of this document, do you know what this means? You will have no say in anything, and I can walk away with everything. All I have to do is give my attorney permission to go to the judge and tell the judge you are in default and you're done for. I want a court date by tomorrow or you will be in default." By that afternoon, a court date was set.

One of the most interesting things that happened during the divorce process was when we both sat down with our attorneys, all together, to work out financial and child visitation details. It was cordial, not antagonistic. We were discussing alimony payments and I had a list of what I spend on a monthly basis. From my point of view, it was reasonable. I was not an extravagant person who threw money away. Oscar was making a very good salary and I was asking for about 20 percent of what he made a year. He wanted to give me 10 percent. Quite a drop in income compared to what I was used to. By the way, this included child support for my daughter who decided to live with me. At the end of the meeting, Oscar's attorney stood up, turned to Oscar, and said, "You're very lucky, your wife is frugal." Cha-ching!! Validation.

My father taught me well about how to manage money, and coming from a blue-collar family with not much money to spare, I knew I would be financially OK. I was also working part-time to supplement my income. Money was only important to me as a means of survival, as a way of putting food on the table and a roof over my head. For me, money was not a reflection of success or happiness, like it was to

Oscar. I was able to make things work financially for myself without depending on anyone else. I was in a much better place financially than most women. Everything was pretty much divided evenly, right down to the kids. But he saw it differently. He felt he was raked over the coals.

Working with battered women, I realized that fighting for custody of the kids only hurts the kids, and a child custody argument is just to get back at the spouse. I was not going to do that to my kids. My son chose to live with his dad and my daughter chose to live with me. My son's decision broke my heart, but I knew I had to let him go and support his choice. For years after the divorce, I couldn't think or talk about him living with his dad because it brought me to tears. But I knew deep down inside of me, that if we were going to have a good relationship, I had to support his decision to be with his father and suffer in silence.

Chapter 21

JUNE 3, 1998, REDEMPTION DAY— RECLAIMING "ME"

The day of my divorce, my dad drove me to the courthouse. I asked him to drive me because the courthouse was in an area that was not safe, or I just did not feel safe. It was reminiscent of NYC. I felt I made it out of the marriage, to some degree unscathed; however, I was unsure I would make it in or out of the courthouse alive. It was much more insignificant than NYC, but probably just as bleak and creepy as NYC. To me, the streets of Paterson were just as threatening and unsafe. The feeling of weakness and trepidation while walking from the parking lot to the entrance of the courthouse, along with the possibility of getting lost and not being able to find the courthouse, created this weight, a boulder, sitting on my chest, feeling my heart pounding in my ears. I wanted to appear strong in court, and driving to the courthouse, alone, with all my disconcerting emotions to keep me company, was not something I wanted to present to the judge or to Oscar.

I knew my father would not object to driving me. Although I never had his emotional support, he was a reasonable man, and I knew he would not let me down. He wanted me to be safe and he knew I was quite apprehensive about going into Paterson. But, in a conversation I had with my dad years later, he said that driving me to the courthouse on the day of my divorce was his way of being supportive. I was grateful that he drove me; however, this "action" of driving me was just that. It was an action and not emotional support, which was something I desperately needed.

Most people would think that driving me to the courthouse *was* being emotionally supportive. This is not true. When I was going through the process of getting divorced, my father would say to me, "How can you divorce him and take all his money?" This was more of a projection on his part because he would never divorce my mother, fearing she would "take all his money." In addition, my mother empathized with Oscar and felt sorry for him. For example, two months before the divorce became finalized, she wanted to invite him to Easter dinner. She must have forgotten about his six siblings and his mother; they were always entertaining for the holidays. The thought never entered her mind that it would be uncomfortable for me to spend a holiday with him. She was only thinking about how bad he was feeling. But I told her that if she invited him for Easter dinner, I would not be attending. She never extended the invitation to him. This was an action on her part but I did not feel any emotional support from either of them.

We had to be at the courthouse at nine in the morning. We had to wait in the hallway as we arrived early. "Waiting" is not something that I do very well. In my family, "patience" was not a virtue that we possessed. It was taxing on me. There were people all around talking, scuffling about, when suddenly the police got our attention, speaking loudly to quickly move to one side, as prisoners in orange jumpsuits, chains around their waists, nice shiny bracelets around their wrists, along with the ankle bracelets, were being escorted through the hallways. Get me the hell out of here, I screamed to myself; I realized the reality, the seriousness, of what takes place in a courthouse.

Nine o'clock arrived and we proceeded into the courtroom. We entered this enclosed, windowless, intolerable room, with an ominous police presence. It appeared dingy and lifeless. Uncomfortable wooden seats, like church, and a feeling that maybe a crucifixion would be a better option than being in divorce court. However, Jesus was not there, no image of him on the cross. But at that moment, I felt that I would be the next person to get nailed (I was so naïve to the process, that I felt the judge would overrule everything that Oscar and I had agreed upon.) I had a sense of the doors locking behind me with no way out. My only perception of a courtroom was what I saw on television: the judge's bench, the jury box, and the spectator seats. We sat in the spectator seats, waiting for the judge to appear. Most surprising and interesting was seeing people I knew from my hometown also going through a divorce. People that I had no previous idea about were experiencing the same situation.

The bailiff cried out, "Please rise," and, just like being in church, we all rose in unison. I was waiting for everyone to genuflect. My anxiety took over and for a moment, I dissociated and I was back in church as a child, waiting for the altar boys to ring the bell and for the smell of incense to take over. I fought the feeling of dizziness and my eyes rolling back into my head to prevent myself from fainting. I, suddenly, realized I am not that child in church; I am a grown woman in court waiting to be granted a divorce.

The judge announced, "All couples that have unresolved issues, proceed to mediation." The court empties out, and all who are left are me, my dad, my attorney, Oscar, and his attorney. I followed my attorney to the front of the court, as directed by the judge. We sat on the left side. In my mind, typically, the plaintiff sits on the right side and the defendant sits on the left. The only thought I had at that moment was "This is the side that OJ sat on."

The judge focused on me first. He asked me my name, where I lived, how long I had been married, and the names and dates of birth of my children. That's when I froze, stiff and paralyzed, unable to process my children's names and when they were born. But I pulled myself together and answered his questions. Then it was Oscar's turn to answer the same questions. And in a matter of minutes, it was all over. There was no gavel that came down, there was no "In the state of New Jersey, I now pronounce you never to like each other again." There was no ripping up the marriage license in court. And there was no music playing Gloria Gaynor's song "I Will Survive," which honestly should be played in divorce court. As a matter of fact, that song became my theme song from that time forward.

After two and a half years and nearly nine thousand dollars, in a matter of minutes, it was done. My attorney turned to me and said, "You *are* going to therapy today, right?" as my anxiety was palpable. I was now on my own, alone, but I was free. Free to be who I wanted to be, needed to be. Free to be me!

Chapter 22

EMPTY NEST IS NOT ALWAYS A BAD THING

The evening of my divorce, I had my security blanket. June had called to see how everything went and to give me emotional support. Genuine emotional support. The sense of unconditional acceptance was something I became accustomed to. She had known me before, during, and after therapy, and the degree of love, caring, and support toward me never faltered. However, I was literally on my own now and had to learn to depend on myself even more. I promised myself I would not go to my parents for any help, because the backlash would have been intolerable. I had to survive solely on my own, as the lyrics to "I Will Survive" continued to resonate in my head.

During the summer of 1998, Bernadette was living with me and graduated from high school. She was also preparing to go off to college. The house was quiet, which was fine, and I felt much closer to my daughter than I ever had before. There were no distractions, not having to confer with her dad about parenting decisions. I always had boundaries with my kids, and she easily abided by those boundaries. I needed to know where she was and what time she thought she would be coming home. If she was going to be late, she had to call. There were no issues. We understood each other. But as August approached and as she prepared herself for leaving the family home, my life would again change.

I hated sleeping alone in the house, fearing someone would break in. But something unexpected happened that was not obviously apparent at first. From the day I received my divorce decree, my nightmares had completely disappeared. The nightmares that I experienced as far back as I could remember, finally evaporated, along with the criticism and control. I no longer had to rely on people who were both unreliable and who disappointed me over and over again. I realized, finally, that not only did I have to rely on myself, but most importantly that I *could* rely on myself. That enhanced sense of control most likely was the unconscious process that diminished the nightmares I suffered with for so many years. I now possessed a sense of freedom and control. My life was finally my own, for me to decide what I want to do and when I want to do it.

The day Bernadette left for college was another emotional milestone. I was unsure of how to get to the college and I asked Oscar if I could go with him, which he was fine with. Moving her into her dorm was uneventful but also heartfelt. My firstborn was, in some way, on her own, starting a new chapter in her life. It was a similar experience to when my son went to live with his father but also different. This was a normal developmental stage that most children go through. My son leaving me was premature.

The drive home was quiet as I was consumed with my own thoughts about her being at college and me truly living alone. I decided I was not going to call her for a few days, as I wanted to give her some space, and I would wait until she reached out to me. That waiting was the most difficult for me.

As I entered my house, I felt a sense of eeriness looming, in what used to be a place full of kids talking, laughing, and arguing, along with the TV blaring in the background. Now, it was just plain quiet. The first thing I had to do was decide what to make for dinner. The second thing was realizing dinner was *my* decision and I thought to myself, "I'm confused, dinner is *rarely* my decision." For decades, dinner was made to satisfy everyone, making green vegetables for one child, carrots for another, and absolutely no onions in anything for Oscar. I continued to think, "Wow, I can have a frozen dinner or any vegetable I want, or I can do takeout." As I debated what I should eat, my phone rang. It was my daughter just wanting to say hi. At that moment I realized some things were still the same. Hearing her voice allowed me to exhale. The ventilation of my lungs expressing an outflow of gases that had built up inside of me since I left the campus now felt like a warm spring breeze that swirled around me, encapsulating me, allowing my body to completely relax. I had thought I would not hear from her for days. I did not lose my daughter.

The next morning when I woke up there was another surprise waiting for me. As I opened the hamper and before I dropped my clothes in, I was able to see the bottom of the hamper, something I had never seen before. It was as if it was brand new, the way I brought it home from the store years ago and unpacked it from the box. It was so clean, pure, and unadulterated. I thought: "Maybe I should get my eyes checked. Am I delusional?" Reality eventuality set in, and I reminded myself that this is what it means to live alone. And then I thought, "Damn, I can get used to this."

Chapter 23

"THAT'S WHAT FRIENDS ARE FOR"

—DIONNE WARWICK

My daughter was at school, my son was living with his father, and I was left to ponder my new life. I was emotionally and financially in a very good place, even though Oscar's alimony check was late almost every month. I decided not to go through probation as I knew he would not skip out on his payments. Like my mother, he was vain and wouldn't do anything to make himself look bad. I also understood how tight he was with money and considering he had to kiss every dollar goodbye, it made sense that the money would not arrive on time. But it wasn't much of a big deal because I was never one to live paycheck to paycheck. I knew how to budget.

I ran into my neighbor one day and told her that we were divorced. She was quite surprised, which actually surprised me. I said, "You didn't notice his car was gone?" She said, "I thought he was on a business trip." Little did she know how much she validated what I had been saying to Oscar for twenty years regarding the frequency of his business trips and how often I was left alone to raise my kids by myself. It validated my own feelings of loneliness within the marriage. This didn't build "character" as he often told me. It built strength and allowed me to follow my own dreams.

A few years back, after I served Oscar with divorce papers, I paid a visit to my neighbor on the other side of my house. As I entered the house, I told them that I had something to tell them. My neighbor looked at me and said, "Are you getting a divorce?" Obviously, they weren't surprised. They didn't say much about what they observed about my marriage. I came to realize that people are not stupid and are very observant, even if they don't say anything about what they have seen. However, the neighbors who showed the most emotion were the neighbors directly across the street. Divorce frightens people, mainly because they realize it can happen to anyone; no one is immune.

I believe one of the most important lessons from divorce is not to make the same mistake twice. Many people fall into the same type of relationship as they had before, without processing why they married the person they did the first time around, and what their participation in the failed marriage was. With all the therapy I had experienced when I divorced, I was ready for a positive relationship with someone who would love me for who I am, take an interest in me, and support me for what I believe in.

While I was going through my divorce, one of my professors from undergrad called me and asked me if I would be interested in being on a panel to speak to undergrads about what it is like to be in graduate school. I am not one for public speaking and usually shy away from being in front of an audience, but I figured this would not be a difficult topic to talk about. Grad school was easy for me because undergrad had prepared me well for Fordham. By the time I graduated from Fordham, I was so burned out from nine years of school that I stopped reading my assignments for class and still maintained a GPA of somewhere around 3.9.

After the panel convened, my college BaFa BaFa professor started to talk to me on a more personal level. It was a couple of years since we were in touch, and the only other time I reached out to him was shortly after I started grad school because I needed help with research methods. He told me he was divorced, and I described what the divorce process was like in New Jersey since he was divorced in New York. As we parted company on that day, I felt a sense of comfort and calmness. My thoughts at that time were not focused on getting into another relationship. I was overwhelmed with my divorce in addition to living with Oscar while going through the divorce, working, going to school, and raising the kids. I could not complicate my life anymore by having someone else enter my life. My main goal was helping my kids through this heartbreaking time.

I liked Marshall. He always seemed calm and rational. I never observed him as being critical in class, like some other professors were. Even though seeing someone new would be hard for the kids, for me, I was ready to start a new life. I had not been in love with Oscar for ten years prior. So, after Bernadette went to college, I reached out to Marshall.

It was scary for me because all I knew was "no one could be trusted" and he seemed "too good to be true," which became a red flag for me. For years to come, I waited for the other shoe to drop, because when something is too good to be true, it usually is. Also, working with battered women and knowing that abusers are always very charming and cajoling at first, I was very skeptical. But he was not "fake charming." He was genuine, he was real. He was who he was, and he did not portray himself as someone he wasn't.

However, on some level, I was skeptical even though I had known him for about four years. In undergrad, I was able to get close to a couple of professors and get to know them, so I had a sense of where he was coming from. I was not completely blind going into this relationship. But my red flag was always waving in the breeze, barely waving, as I knew he was a feminist, which comforted me. It was years later when I realized that he was the male version of June, like being in "comfortable sweats" all day long. When I reached out to him, we decided it was time to go out. We went out to a playhouse in Nyack on our first date. Being with him was exciting, scary, and easy all at the same time.

This relationship was something that I had never experienced with anyone else. We talked for hours, about everything and it was easy and freeing. I did not feel vulnerable; I did not have to hide my feelings. I could tell him anything and everything. He listened without judgment and took his time to understand who I was. I did not have to be perfect or behave in a way that my mother or Oscar wanted me to behave and approved of, which was impossible for me to do. With Marshall, I could just be "me." There were no concerns about him using anything I said against me in public. He was accepting of me. He became my best friend. And one thing about best friends, they will always have your back and not turn on you. However, these mixed emotions wreaked havoc within me, as this new way of communicating with someone was unfamiliar and confusing for me. I was in unknown territory; uncharted waters. As comforting as it was, it was also disturbing to me. It was not that I was waiting for the "other shoe to drop." I was waiting for the high-speed collision on a major highway to occur. The collision when you are driving seventy miles an hour and all of a sudden, the tractor-trailer in front of you stops. All I could visualize was my car smashing into this truck, getting wedged underneath the back of the truck, and not being able to extract myself from it. It happens so fast that one is unable to see it coming, nor is it preventable. The hood of the car becomes wedged underneath the truck and, like with a guillotine, your head is chopped off. I could fantasize it happening one day. Sneaking up on me in a way that I was not prepared for. I did not want that to happen. I felt I was too old, too tired, and had too much life experience to be put in that position again. So, my red flag was always waving in the breeze, but it was more like a banner than a flag.

However, as time went on, my red flag started to turn green, and all my insecurities about trusting him started to wane. We saw each other frequently, and as time passed, I had less apprehension about the relationship.

In this relationship, nothing ever seemed to be a big deal. He was always more interested in what I wanted and needed rather than putting his needs first. When we went out to dinner, I insisted on paying my half, as I never wanted to feel obligated to anyone. But there were many times when he insisted on paying for my dinner. He knew I was on a limited budget and was concerned about that and wanted *me* to avoid tuna fish. However, it is Marshall's favorite thing to eat.

Chapter 24

AGAIN WITH THE MOTHER

By April of 1999, Marshall and I decided to buy a house together, but he would not move in until August. He had been living rent-free on campus since his divorce, and I guess the agreement he had with the college was for him to move out prior to the new semester.

In May of that year, I graduated from Fordham, sold my house, bought a house, sat for the state exam that allowed me to call myself a social worker, and was hired to work on a locked psych unit where I received my clinical experience. This happened all in a matter of a few weeks.

I never told my parents ahead of time that I was selling my house and buying another until it actually happened. I wanted to avoid hearing the negativity and how I shouldn't, couldn't, or was incapable of doing it. I never told them that Marshall and I bought the house together and that he was moving in until he actually moved in. I was forty-five years old at that time, it was 1999—nearly the turn of the century, the millennium, and more than thirty years since the women's rights movement began. But my mother was appalled, disgusted, and embarrassed by the thought of her daughter "living in sin." How could I possibly do this to her? By this point in my life, I no longer cared about what she thought of me, and I no longer cared about her feelings. Since my family had sided with Oscar, I was pretty much done with them.

But my mother was vindictive. While we were living together and even though Marshall is Jewish, she decided not to give him a Christmas present on Christmas Day, nor did she give him a birthday present until we were married. Marshall was not bothered by this at all, but it was the proverbial "knife in the back" for me. It was once again "I will control you, and if you refuse to listen, there will be consequences." What my mother did not comprehend was that her quasi-punishment no longer had the impact that it did when I was fifteen years old. Marshall was my "safe haven," and I no longer feared my mother.

A few months after Marshall moved in, we talked about a wedding. We wanted a destination wedding, before it actually became a thing. It was just a matter of where the wedding would take place. One of the nurses at the hospital suggested Key West and gave me the name of a hotel where she had once stayed. We went to the local travel agency and sat down with Lynn, who became our travel agent for the next twenty-five years.

We decided we would marry on the first day of spring of the new millennium. We flew our kids down to join us in the ceremony and stay for a few days. Marshall also has a daughter and son about ten years older than my kids. Our parents did not come. His parents were much older than my parents, and it would have been more of a hardship on them than anything else, and my parents—well, my mother—refused to fly. Not having my parents there was more of a relief than anything else.

We married in Key West and two and a half months later we had a celebration with our friends and family in the clubhouse at our townhouse complex. On the day of the party celebrating our union together, as we were greeting our guests, my sister came, surprisingly, without my parents. She approached me and told me they were not coming because Mom had a migraine. Honestly, I have never known my mom to have migraines; I thought she only gave people migraines. I was pissed off but not surprised. Probably a bit more than pissed off. What was going through her head? She wanted me married to avoid feeling any responsibility for me; however, being married to a psychologist was even more threatening to her. Being married, again, meant my mother had even less control than before, as Marshall was a very different person. As a matter of fact, my father had told me he had never seen me as relaxed and happy as I was with Marshall. But this was a double-edged sword for my mother. She would not be able to influence Marshall; he was not Oscar! She was more afraid of him, fearing he would analyze her. However, after an hour or so, my parents showed up for the party. I barely acknowledged their presence.

Chapter 25

MY BROTHER'S CONTROL WAS OUT OF CONTROL

The less I depended on my family, the less I needed them, the more intense it became with them. I became more outspoken with my family and no longer swallowed and internalized what they said to me. I fought back, which created lots of issues. I disrupted the equilibrium of the family unit. I started to verbalize to Dominic how I felt about my mother. Even though he knew what she was like, he was unable to handle what I was saying. Dominic, as much as he agreed with me with respect to their behavior, still needed and relied on them much more than I ever did. Soon enough, Dominic and I would become estranged for a long time.

I was godmother to his first child and his son's birthday was approaching. Two weeks before his birthday, my mother was talking to me about the birthday party. I had said, "I didn't get an invitation." I waited and waited. I said to Marshall, "If my sister-in-law calls the night before, I will not attend the party." The night before my nephew's birthday, my sister-in-law called, and I decided not to pick up the phone and let it go to voicemail. I continued to be surprised that my family betrayed me and forgot about me. I was probably still hoping for their approval and inclusion, to feel like I was part of this dysfunctional family unit. But I was furious and in a frenzy. I felt out of control. My thoughts swirled around in my head, like confetti, flying around in circles, not being able to grab onto one piece to help make sense as to why I was not invited until hours before. It still baffled me as to why I had been treated like an outsider.

It was the yearly family vacation, all over again, that my brother organized and didn't invite me to. The vacation my brother organized with my sister and my parents that I was excluded from. The yearly vacation to Wildwood that he organized, without giving me a second thought. The vacation that I was told about, not invited to, but was told about an hour before they were leaving for the beach, as I sat home with my kids, while my husband traveled to Europe on business.

I prevented myself from becoming impulsive with my response, so I let it sit overnight. I wanted to be comfortable about what I was going to say to my sister-in-law. I called her the next morning and said the following: "I will not be attending. I am extremely hurt that you waited hours before the party to invite me when everyone else was invited two weeks ago." We hung up. Once again, I was not important enough to be given the courtesy of an invitation ahead of time. Dominic called me about ten minutes later, screaming like a lunatic, cursing like I had never heard before. Sailors would have been embarrassed and appalled. He told me he "disowned" me, I am no longer his sister, and he never wants to see me again. By the time I got off the phone, I was shaking, quivering. He was abusive and the most out of control I'd ever seen him. This was the last straw for me. It took me decades to see who my brother really was, and I despised what I saw; I detested who he had become. And this was all because I made him accountable. It was all because I expressed how I felt about the last-minute invitation.

I called my mother, why I don't know, and Dominic had called her just moments before to tell her what had happened. My mother had little to say about it, and I knew she would not go against her son. But what happened going forward was most interesting. My brother, who rarely if ever hosted holidays or dinner parties, decided to have every holiday at his house with my parents. That meant I was alone for every holiday. I, at first, was crushed, but then, similar to when I first got divorced, it was OK. I no longer had to do all the cooking and prep prior to the holidays. The first Christmas I spent without my family was hard but not awful. Dominic monopolized my parents in order to avoid me having access to them on holidays and also to appear as "the good child." Even Christmas Eve my parents spent with Dominic.

But there was one Christmas Eve my mother invited us over. On that Christmas Eve, we (my daughter and my husband) were there for about an hour when my father said to my mother, "What time is *he* coming over?" I looked at my parents and said: "What, you invited him? I told you I would only come over if he wasn't coming. If he is coming,

I am leaving." My mother panicked and begged me not to leave, and my father's famous words to me were "Don't be like that." My father was unable to deal with the conflict, and his way of resolving disputes was to just give in and not discuss and process the problem. As I tried to present my case in front of the panel of judges (my parents) again, they were not having it. I turned to my husband and daughter and said, "Get the coats, we are leaving." At that point, my mother became more upset saying, "Don't leave, please don't leave, he's going to apologize and make everything right." I said: "Oh really, why now, just because he's alone for Christmas Eve? He could've called me at any time to apologize. He's a coward, all he wants is your support, that's why he's doing this today. He knows you both will side with him. You either call him now and tell him not to come or we are leaving." My mother called him and told him not to come. We ended up staying, but the emotions I experienced were, again, familiar: outrage, disappointment, and betrayal. I felt a deep sense of sadness and I just wanted to go home and be left alone. Whenever I thought they had done the worst thing they could possibly do, I became more surprised at their behavior. This was the worst Christmas Eve ever.

Diane Harth

Chapter 26

THE LONGER THE ESTRANGEMENT, THE STRONGER I BECAME

Dominic and I did not speak for several years. The longer our estrangement went on, the better I felt. I had less stress and anxiety. I never felt that there was a void in my life or that something was missing. It was one less family member I had to deal with. My parents never talked about him and neither did my sister.

My mother and I had several arguments during that time; I have little to no recollection of their nature. It was probably the usual stuff my mother would complain about—"You don't call me enough, you don't visit enough, you don't do enough for me." One day we had a blowup, and I refused to call her. After a week or so, my dad called to tell me how much she was suffering over this. Mind you, if she's suffering, *he* is suffering. My sister would call and say, "Call Mom." That was it, no other words were spoken. No one was capable of tolerating her bitching and moaning, and no one ever held her accountable. They were all afraid of her. But I was not going to cave. I would not call.

One day when I was out, Marshall signed for a registered letter for me from my mother. I was pissed because if I had answered the door, I never would have signed for it. I threw the letter out after a few days after I showed it to my therapist. My therapist suggested I write a letter to her explaining how I felt. Before I sent my response letter to her, I read it to my therapist. I guess I was looking for approval and wanted to make sure I wasn't provoking her in any way. I sent the letter off with all my grievances.

My mother eventually called me and accused me of not writing the letter and accused Marshall of writing the letter. The letter was very well-written, as I gathered my thoughts and communicated my feelings without attacking her. I stated the facts. But when she accused me of not writing it, I thought to myself, does this shit ever stop? They still saw me as a stupid child. I had a master's degree, the only one on my mother's side and my father's side of the family to reach that level of education. But that was irrelevant.

My mother was unable to tolerate arguing with me and realized I was not going to give in to her narcissistic tendencies anymore. As always, nothing ever got resolved, and we just went about our business, trying not to upset each other. But I drifted even further away from her.

Chapter 27

NEW YEAR'S EVE 2003

I became content and accustomed to my life and not speaking to Dominic. My theory about Dominic's behavior was twofold. He saw me disconnecting, breaking away from the family, and most likely was upset with himself that he was not strong enough to do the same. My brother was never financially secure. He spent money as if he had a trust fund, which got him into major financial trouble. He made poor financial decisions and turned to my parents to help him out. Out of the three of us, I was the only one who was responsible with money, as my parents managed my sister's money. I was the only one who was both emotionally and financially independent. I can hypothesize that my personal and financial independence made him envious. He was also unhappy in his marriage, and I freely, independently, left my marriage, without the help and support of my parents. "I" made that decision on my own. My sister's divorce was not her decision; it was Dominic's decision, and my parents followed his lead. I imagine that Dominic, seeing how emotionally strong I was, was infuriated, considering I never had the support of the family. He did not have that kind of stamina, courage, and sense of independence to leave his wife at that time.

Two thousand four was to be a year that changed the family's lives. Marshall and I never went out for New Year's Eve. Even today, we watch movies on TV, get takeout, and stay off the streets to avoid all the drunks. On December 31, 2003, the moment the clock hit midnight, as we watched on TV the ball dropping in Times Square, I had this insurmountable, nauseating, distressful feeling that penetrated throughout my body to the degree that I could not contain it. I had to share this feeling even though I had no scientific evidence that it would become a reality. I looked at Marshall and said: "I can't explain this, and I know you are going to think I'm crazy, but I have this feeling that I've never had before that is just gnawing at me. I can't get rid of it. I feel something terrible is going to happen this year and I don't know what it is." He said, "What do you mean, what kind of terrible thing?" I told him I didn't know, but the discomfort I felt was real and I couldn't shake it. For days after, Marshall kept questioning me about these feelings that remained inside of me like a disease, like a leach that I could not disconnect from.

But life went on. I remember having a conversation with my sister, who *never* went to a doctor because if you go to a doctor, they will find something wrong with you. I encouraged her to go to my gynecologist for an exam. Surprisingly, she went, and he sent her for a mammogram. And then life changed. She was diagnosed with stage four breast cancer. At that time, to my knowledge, no one in the family was ever diagnosed with cancer, and this came as a shock to everyone. I have no idea why I had that conversation with my sister.

However, unconsciously there had to be something that was percolating below my level of awareness with respect to my sister's health. It still puzzles me to this day.

My parents, understandably, were distraught. However, I knew they would also be useless and had limited knowledge of medicine. I would not say I was proficient in the medical field, but I am married to someone who has a much better understanding of medicine. His mother worked in a hospital as an EEG technician and his daughter is a neurologist. Marshall is also very smart, as he did research on animal behavior along with performing surgery at times on birds, which probably should not go unmentioned. He also did have substantial research experience that could help in the process of making decisions. I, therefore, was able to gain access to information and knew the questions to ask the doctors. At that point, I became involved with my sister's care and attended most, if not all, of her doctor appointments. I knew my parents would not be able to process anything the doctors said, primarily because they were so upset and because they would not understand most of the medical terminology involved. I would go to as many doctor appointments as possible and just take notes. I was a fourth set of ears in the room and probably the only ones that were fully functioning.

Within a few months, I needed a hysterectomy. Of course, this didn't fit into my mother's busy schedule of cleaning, cooking, and food shopping. She told me she couldn't come to the hospital every day but would be there when I got out of surgery. I remember waking up in the

OR and my doctor asking me questions to make sure I was oriented to person, place, and time. I passed that test. I also remember being rolled down the hallways and approaching my room. The first person I saw was my husband, who had a stuffed animal in his hands. He immediately kissed me and held my hand. Then I saw my parents, which was uneventful. After my parents left, he told me something that he was shocked and appalled about, which I did not find surprising at all. He went to the gift shop to buy me a gift. When he saw my parents, he told them about what he found in the gift shop in case they wanted to buy me something. He said my mother's response was "Why the hell would I want to buy her something?" Even though he knew what my parents were like, this was not his life experience. He told me his eyes rolled back into his head and he was absolutely flabbergasted by her response.

I looked forward to the respite in the hospital. My doctor decided to arrange for me to have a private room. Once again, I anticipated and predicted my mother's behavior, and she never disappointed me in that respect. I was in the hospital for about two to three days. I had drains coming out of me and was catheterized because I had a prolapsed bladder that the doctor had fixed as part of the hysterectomy procedure. My mother called me, and I was all prepared. After a five-second check on how I was doing, she asked me if I could talk to my doctor about my sister's cancer. I said to her, "Mom, I just had major surgery, she has her own doctors and I need to focus on my own recovery." And that was when the phone call ended.

But that was not the first time my surgery was not a priority. In 2002, I had emergency gallbladder surgery. I had been in pain for a few weeks and wasn't sure what was causing it. I thought it would just go away, but the pain persisted. My husband picked me up from work one day because my car was being serviced. The pain was so bad I told him to take me to the ER. I told him to call my mother to let her know. The emergency room staff immediately did an ultrasound. My experience with something like this has been that when asking the technician, sometimes they say, "It's fine." But this time she said, "The doctor will talk to you." I knew something was wrong. The technician left and now Marshall, doctors, and nurses were in the room. I'm half naked as they were doing an EKG and someone came into the room and asked if there was a Dr. Harth there. Bear in mind, it was twelve midnight at this point. Marshall looked at me inquisitively and I said, "It's probably my mother." And sure enough, it was. He talked to her for a few minutes, and I saw this pained look on his face as he did not want to be disrespectful. I told him to give me the phone. My mother said to me: "Why do they have to do surgery immediately? I don't have time to be at the hospital tomorrow for you" (as if I needed her to do the surgery). She continued on, "I have to take your sister to the doctor tomorrow." What my mother was not able to realize was that there was no need for her to be at the hospital. I also did not want her at the hospital. I had all the support I needed. I had my kids on speed dial, as they were both in college, and I had my husband by my side.

Chapter 28

THE HIGHER MOM'S ANXIETY WAS, THE MORE INAPPROPRIATE SHE BECAME

Originally, I had suggested to my parents that they take my sister to Memorial Sloan Kettering Cancer Center in NYC. They said absolutely not. It wasn't until the very end of her life when Dominic suggested it, when it was too late, did they take her to Sloan. I always wondered if things would have worked out differently had they agreed to go to Sloan from the start.

I had called my gynecologist and asked him for a referral for a breast surgeon. My sister's cancer was environmental and not genetic. That was confirmed not only by the doctors but also when I took the BRCA test a few years later. My sister was scheduled for a mastectomy. The day of her surgery, my parents, Marshall, and I were at the hospital. They prepped her for surgery and my mom, Marshall, and I went in to wait with her until they were ready to bring her down to the OR. My dad sat in the waiting room. I believe it was too painful for him to be there with her. As we sat, my mother blurted out, "You can't believe the dream I had last night." My husband, the psychologist, and I both looked at each other, and he looked at her and said, "What was it about?" She must have realized who she was talking to and immediately said, "Oh no, I'm not telling you." Later that day, Marshall and I both laughed about it.

The nurse came in and said they were ready for my sister. My mother looked at my sister and said a four-letter word that I had never heard her say in my entire life: "love." She said to her, "I love you." I was unaware that my mother was even familiar with that word. My mother had said four-letter words before but never that word. We followed behind the gurney to the OR. To me, it was a very familiar scene, except this time, I was vertical and not horizontal looking up at the bright lights. We got to the OR holding area and were allowed to stay with her until the surgeon spoke to us, before they brought her into the OR itself. He explained how long it would take and also the procedure, the details of which have escaped my memory. What I do remember was my mother asking question after question until my sister said the following, which at the time was pretty damn funny. She said, "Mom, don't piss him off, he has a knife and will be cutting into me."

The surgery went fine, and my sister appeared in good spirits. The next day, I went to visit her in the hospital. My mother, who had no couth or sense of decorum whatsoever, within five minutes of me being there said the following: "Go ahead, Trish, show her your boob." I was not surprised at my mother's insensitivity but was blown away at the same time. Who does that? Who says that? I felt embarrassed for my sister. But my sister, willing to please Mom, said to me, "I will show you if you want." I have to say I was curious but *never* would have asked to see what it looked like. That was very private and personal. But that was my mother. I believe it was my mother's own anxiety that prompted her to say that. She needed to hear from *me* (not sure why since I'm the stupid one) that everything looked OK (like I was a doctor giving my professional opinion). Honestly, I was not upset by the appearance of her breast.

However, the bad news continued after her breast surgery. About two months after her surgery, my sister was diagnosed with another primary cancer. Bladder cancer. What I found out was months before she was diagnosed with breast cancer, she had blood in her urine and did nothing about it. Back in 2004, they removed the bladder, but it is my understanding that doctors don't do that as frequently today. My sister had an ostomy bag for the rest of her life.

I continued going to as many doctor appointments as possible. Her oncologist was about five minutes from the hospital where I worked. On one occasion, I had agreed to meet my family there for her four-thirty appointment. I got out of work at four o'clock and figured I had plenty of time. However, I did not expect road construction and detours. I knew my mother was going to have a shit fit if I wasn't there when she expected and wanted me to be there. And I was late, "very late," according to my mother. I made it there by four-thirty, in time for the appointment. According to my mother, I was late because I wasn't there early. As I arrived in the parking lot, I saw my father pacing back and forth—*in the parking lot*—like a nervous cat in a room full of rocking chairs. I got out of the car and in a very calm voice he said to me, "Your mother is a wreck, you're late, she sent me out to look for you." I thought to myself, "As if that would make me be here any sooner." I told him all the roads were blocked for some reason and I got there as soon as I could. I entered the waiting room. There were one or two other people there, and my mother proceeded to yell at me for being late as if I was still a teenager. I sat there and ignored her. But what I felt inside of myself was quite different. I felt my body, my organs, break up into tiny parts, as if a missile shot through me. I was spontaneously disintegrating before my own eyes. The emotional strength I always depended on exited my body, leaving me feeling weak and depleted. The cohesiveness, the equilibrium, between my body and mind no longer existed, I felt a complete breakdown emotionally and physically. I was humiliated and drained, as I felt the blood drain from my body.

I had to pull myself together for this appointment and put on my social worker cap. I needed to be disconnected from my family in order to comprehend what the doctor was saying. Luckily, I had a therapy appointment that evening; therefore, it was easier for me to hold it together. After the appointment I rejected my mother; I gave her the silent treatment. She made me feel ashamed. I could not look at her or speak to her. I got in my car and left.

I got to my therapy appointment, and the minute my therapist looked at my face she knew something was wrong. She sat there staring at me as I described what had happened. She had her thumb underneath her chin, as her face rested on the other three fingers while her index finger was up against her right cheek. As I described what my mother did and how I felt, I could almost picture what was going through her head by her flat affect. The flat affect always kicks in during serious disclosures. I vented for the entire session. We talked about some options on how to deal with my mother. I decided I was not going to speak with her right away. I needed time, distance.

When I step back and think about my parents' border-line behavior, I find the "You're a good enough daughter, you're not a good enough daughter" dichotomy fascinating. I was essential to their ability to survive emotionally, intellectually, and practically. They needed my ability to navigate the stresses of my sister's cancer, which they were unable to comprehend emotionally or cognitively. They were desperate for my help but incapable of overtly acknowledging it. They were incapable of allowing me to feel good about what I was doing not only for them but also for my sister. I was useful to them, good enough in some instances, and not good enough for them in other instances.

Chapter 29

THE SECOND SADDEST DAY OF MY LIFE

I refrained from speaking to my mother for several days, and frankly, I would have been happy to never speak to her again. Her behavior was inappropriate, and I am sure the other people in the waiting room who observed it were just as uncomfortable as I was. Once again, my dad called and wanted to know why I had not called her. I told him the phone works both ways, and if she wants to speak to me, she would have to call me as I am not calling her. My dad knew why I was upset, as he was in the waiting room when she blew up at me. But my dad always defended her, stating it was hard for her to see her daughter suffer with cancer. It was hard to deny that. However, I asked him how he could explain the one million other times she behaved like an ass toward me. My mother did eventually call me. There was no apology from her, and I had nothing to apologize for, and life went on the way it always did. I did have some compassion for her. Her child had cancer, and I knew early on that it was not going to end well. My mother had no clue what stage four cancer meant, and my sister's doctors were not going to tell my parents and my sister what it really meant. With that being said, this was only the first year of her treatment, and, to be fair, anything could happen.

After my sister recovered from her surgeries, she decided to do chemo. She was still working, and her boss was very good to her. As a matter of fact, at the end of her life when she was on disability, her boss gave her a raise. There are some good people left in this world. But every Thursday she had her treatment, and every Friday she was back at work. I swear my sister had a cast iron stomach. She never, or rarely, got sick from her treatment. She lost all her hair, and I toyed with the idea of shaving my head in solidarity. However, by that time I was in private practice, and I wasn't sure how my clients would react.

Her chemo was an all-day thing or at least for several hours. My parents would go and sit with her during her treatments but then couldn't handle it anymore. I was working many hours building my practice, but my mother was unable to comprehend why I was unable to be with my sister during her treatment. My mother, who had free time during the day, was unable to manage sitting all day and just watching the chemo go through the IV, but she expected me to take off work and watch the IV. She actually told me what a bad sister I was because I rejected the idea of taking off from work to sit at the cancer center looking at the IV drip for hours. She never acknowledged my job as being important. Dominic, I believe, attended few doctor appointments, and it is my understanding that my mother never asked him to take time off from work to be with my sister on chemo days.

After her surgery and while she was getting her chemotherapy, she had several follow-up doctor appointments. By the end of the summer of 2005, she was admitted to the hospital more frequently. One day my mother called me. She said, "You have to come here immediately." I said, "Why?" She said, "Your sister isn't feeling well." I said, "What are her symptoms?" It was like pulling teeth to get any information out of her. She said she was vomiting. I told her to call 911 and get an ambulance to take her to the hospital. My mom said she was not going to do that and that I had to come over. "Mom, I'm not a doctor, and if I come over, I'm only going to call 911, so either you do it or I do it." Her response was the irrational following: "If she goes to the hospital, they will find something wrong and admit her." I thought to myself, well duh, the woman has cancer and she's sick. My mother eventually called 911.

By the time Thanksgiving came in 2005, my sister was not in good shape. She was again in the hospital. I went to visit her and found out that they were doing another surgery that day. I phoned the secretary of the college to leave a message for Marshall that I would be home late because I was staying at the hospital. My sister told me it was exploratory and probably a hernia. I did not think much of it because I did not have all the information. I had spoken to the doctor before she went into surgery (I had interacted with him several times by now,) and told him, in front of my parents, that he was only to communicate with *me*! She went off to surgery and it was just me and my parents. My mother wanted to go into the chapel and pray and asked if I would go with her. I was so vulnerable at that moment that my mother could have asked me anything and I would have agreed to it—even if she asked me to care for her in her old age. I was in such an emotional state, concerned about my sister's medical condition, that I was unaware that my invisible protective armor, the shield that was constantly around me since birth, had been stripped from my body. This nakedness had allowed me to acquiesce to my mother's request. As I entered the chapel with my mother, it was quiet, primarily because the floors were carpeted, but more so because it was private and nondenominational. Something I wasn't used to. As I entered the room with my mother, I wasn't sure if lightning was going to strike and we would all be blown to bits. Surprisingly, my olfactory system did not kick in and the absence of incense made me feel comfortable. The chapel had an altar, which my mother approached, then kneeled and prayed for my sister's recovery. There were no hard, uncomfortable benches to sit on, as there are in a church. There is something to be said for those uncomfortable pews. I believe religion wants people to feel uncomfortable because when someone is uncomfortable, they look for a higher power to comfort them. When one is comfortable, one can ponder and question that higher power. In this chapel, however, there were very comfortable chairs in which one could relax and look at the stained glass windows above. We stayed for a short while and went back into the waiting room.

I then got called to the reception area. The doctor was on the phone. He told me the cancer had spread throughout her body. I turned away from looking at my parents. I asked him how long she had. He said, "Three months." I asked him if he was going to tell her. He said, "No." I asked him what I should do if she asked me how long she had. He said, "Tell her the truth." *Shit*! In a split second, I decided not to tell my parents that she only had a few months. I went back to where they were sitting, and they wanted to know what the doctor said. I told them the cancer had spread. My mother fell apart, weeping, and my father was stone-faced. I had never seen that look on my father's face before, which scared me. It was a look of terror, sadness, and hopelessness. He was despondent and sullen, in disbelief, hoping I misinterpreted what the doctor said.

The surgery was going to continue for a while. I walked around with my mother who was sobbing, looking to buy her some water. A hospital staffer saw that my mother was in distress and put us in a private room. The three of us just sat there devastated. All I was trying to do was not tell them that the end was near. At this point, my father had not said one word. And then he looked at me and said: "You're hiding something. What else did the doctor say?" I said, "Nothing." He said: "I don't believe you. How long does she have?" My heart was breaking. With all my education and experience working with people, no one taught me how to deal with this. I was unprepared. I felt this incredible pressure with two opposing thoughts running through my head. My first thought was to keep this to myself and bear the burden alone, and the other was to unload this burden, share the burden with them. My dad kept pushing. He finally broke me and I said, "She has three months." It was more than my mother could handle. My dad, in a very low voice, said, "Oh, God." At this point, a doctor needed the room and we had to leave and go back into the waiting room.

I sat with them and told them I had to get some air and I would be back in a few. As I walked out of the hospital, I saw my husband walking toward me. He obviously got my message. I fell into his arms and said nothing. He knew it was bad news.

My sister came out of surgery and was in post-op. Two people were allowed to go in and see her. My dad told me to go in with my mother (he probably knew I was more emotionally equipped to handle her emotions than he was). On some level I think he didn't know how to comfort my mother and didn't know how to act around my sister. My mother and I went in. My sister was completely wired up to monitors and still under anesthesia. My mother started talking to her, and I couldn't believe what I witnessed. I thought this only happened on TV. I nearly burst out laughing. The heart monitor went crazy the moment my mother started talking. I thought I was in a *Seinfeld* episode. My sister, who never said anything negative about my mother, suddenly, unconsciously, and probably the only way she could say something negative about my mother, said it all. It was at this point that she validated what I always believed to be true about my mother. My mother creates an environment of stress and anxiety. The only way my sister could have expressed how my mother affected her, was to be unconscious.

The entire family was at her bedside once they got her into a room, even Dominic and his new girlfriend. He had eventually divorced his wife, which I was not informed about. My mother begged me not to tell my sister how much time she had left. I told my mom that if she asked, I would tell. We were now in the hospital room. My brother and his girlfriend at the foot of the bed, my father and Marshall next to him, my mother sitting in a chair next to her and I am right beside her, holding her hand. The moment she opened her eyes and saw the Addams family looking at her, she knew something was wrong. Before she asked how long she had, my mother started saying in a very loud voice, "Don't tell her." I looked at my mother and said: "Mom, she's sick, not deaf. Stop yelling." I was also thinking, if you don't want her to know, why yell "Don't tell her"? My sister looked at me and asked, "How long do I have?" Again, no one prepares you for this moment. I said, "About three months." She cried but did not get hysterical.

We all stayed for a while and then left. My brother left first, and it was just the four of us. I told my dad I would drive them home in their car and Marshall would follow. My dad was insistent on driving himself home with my mom. After about ten minutes of arguing, Marshall said to my dad, "Your daughter will drive you home," and he said OK.

Chapter 30

PROJECTION

The next morning, I called my father and spoke to him about how to prepare for her death and how to protect whatever money she had. I asked him if she had a will and he said she didn't. I stressed to him the importance of her making up a will to protect any assets she had so the government would not take it when she passed. I told him I could get an attorney to go to the hospital and he could get this done immediately. He just listened and did not respond.

My husband and I went to the hospital that day to visit and Dominic was there. We didn't speak; however, he decided to confront me about the will. "Confront" was an understatement. My father obviously spoke to him after my conversation with him that morning. Basically, my brother told me to stay out of my sister's business and that she was easily influenced and would basically do what anyone wanted her to do. He accused me of wanting to steal her money. The truth of the matter was that my sister's life was run by my parents and Dominic, and they did not want me to sway her away from them. They did not want "me" to influence her the way they had always influenced all her decisions. Dominic was in his own financial turmoil at that point and needed any money he could get his hands on. Additionally, in a subsequent conversation I had with my father, he repeated verbatim what my brother had said. I never spoke about the will again; however, weeks later I was informed that a will had been drawn up. What I find fascinating is that my dad would, on a few occasions, take my advice but never acknowledge that he did till months later.

I knew the entire family was emotionally struggling with this, and I also knew that I was the only sane one in the family despite what I was always told. My parents were completely beside themselves and my brother was too close to my sister to be able to be objective about anything. I was the only one dealing with reality. My parents were in complete denial about her cancer and thought she was going to miraculously recover, regardless of the cancer spreading throughout her body. They could not accept it and could not tolerate or face the truth about her demise.

For me, emotionally, I refused to allow anyone to see me suffer through this. Every morning I would wake up around five and shed my tears into my pillow. I refused to let my husband see me cry. I was fifty-two years old and prohibited myself from crying since I was twelve years old because my mother had said, "Stop crying or I will give you something to cry about." So I stifled my feelings. I suffered in silence for decades. Basically, my mother just could not handle anyone's emotions. I became the strong one, not only for myself but for my parents also.

After this incident at the hospital, I decided if I wanted to see my sister, I would have to visit her when I knew no one would be there. I would get up very early in the morning and be at the hospital around seven. I would stay at the hospital until it was time for me to go to work, since my office was two blocks away. This was very convenient for me. I would then go back to the hospital after I was done with clients at around eight or nine at night. It was a tough schedule; however, I wanted to be with her and I needed to be with her, not only for me but for her. Additionally, my emotional well-being was very important and I had to avoid my family. She was in and out of the hospital until she passed.

I kept my kids posted about their aunt's condition. My son was in college at Boston University and my daughter was living in New Jersey with her husband. My daughter asked me to ask my sister if she could visit her in the hospital. My sister welcomed her niece's visit. When we arrived at the hospital, my daughter wanted to be alone in the room with her. I left the room, and it wasn't long before my daughter came out. She said my sister didn't want to talk. I wasn't surprised. I didn't learn until a year or so later what my daughter wanted to tell my sister. When my daughter gave birth to her firstborn, she named her daughter after my sister. My sister would have been thrilled to learn that her great-niece was named after her.

Chapter 31

THE SADDEST, MOST DIFFICULT DAY OF MY LIFE

Three months had passed since we were given the news about her expected demise. She surpassed the three-month mark, primarily because she did not want to miss the Super Bowl. I think she needed to process why the Giants were not in the Super Bowl! It was the first week of March 2006 and she was back in the hospital. It was a Friday and I was at the hospital with my parents. For the first time since I had known her, the TV was not on. Her hospital room was eerily quiet. This was very strange because my sister was always watching sports on TV. We were sitting in her room and I caught my father's eye. He tilted his head and moved his eyes in the direction of the doorway. I got up and he followed me into the hallway. There happened to be two chairs outside her room where we sat. He looked at me for what seemed to be hours of silence and said, "How does it look to you?" I said, "Do you really want to hear this or is this a rhetorical question?" He nodded in an affirmative way. I said, "She is getting close." He then disclosed to me that I, along with my brother, were made health care proxies for my sister in case my parents weren't able to make decisions. He also told me that they did obtain a lawyer, months ago when I suggested it, to make up a will. Everything had been a secret. One would think they would have told me that back in November. However, no funeral arrangements were made. I will assume that might have been a bridge too far for them. I could understand that; after all, they never accepted her illness.

I spent hours that entire weekend at the hospital. On that Monday morning, around seven, my mother called me to tell me my sister was moved into intensive care. I told her I would go to the hospital to be with her. When I got to the hospital, I had to do a lot of talking to get them to allow me to see her, as it was before visiting hours would begin. Once I was on the ICU, her primary nurse, who was a bitch, told me my sister had been a major pain in the ass all morning. My sister had been vomiting and calling for the nurse every few minutes. And I thought to myself, I have to get this bitch fired. I was directed to put on scrubs and gloves before I entered the room. I entered the room and my sister looked at me. She asked me if she was dying. I had to tell her the truth, I just could not lie to her. I got down close to her and whispered in her ear: "It's time to let go. It's OK, Mom and Dad will be all right. We will all make it through this." She told me to get the nurse because she was having trouble breathing. They immediately got a thoracic surgeon to the room. The doctor walked into the room and my only thought was "God, are you good looking."

My sister told him what the problem was, and he explained how he could relieve the pressure in her chest along with some of the risks. I asked my sister if she understood what the doctor was saying, and she agreed to the procedure. Her breathing was so impaired and created such discomfort, she was not concerned about the risks. I also knew that her time was limited, and the risks were no longer an issue as she was very close to the end. The doctor looked at me and needed my consent to proceed. Luckily for her, I had been appointed her health care proxy in the event my parents were not available.

I left the room and sat in a nearby waiting room. I called my mother and she had asked if Marshall could stay with Trish for a while when I left to attend my class. I was doing post-grad studies at an analytic institute. My mom said they had to go to the attorney's office. I found out later they were putting me back in the will again. I called Marshall and he was able to come and stay with my sister when I left.

As I was sitting in the waiting room, I saw my sister's breast surgeon walk by and I stopped him. He asked what I was doing in ICU and I told him what was going on. He said, "Stay here, I will get back to you." When he returned, he said nothing. What he did was take his right hand with his four fingers pointed at his neck and wave his hand back and forth. I asked how much longer, and he said, "Anytime now, possibly a day or so."

My husband came to the hospital when I left to go to my class so my sister wouldn't be alone. I made a conscious decision not to be present when she died. I'm not sure if that was the right decision or not, but I have no regrets about what I decided to do. I had made my peace with her during one of my visits a few months previously. I said to her, "I have always loved you, and all I wanted was for you to get away from Mom and be independent of her. I was always looking out for your best interest." Her response was interesting, as her sense of humor never left her, not even on her deathbed. She said, "I guess this wasn't how you thought I would get away from her." Unfortunately for her, she didn't have a chance at independence due to my parents' and my brother's hold on her. They never gave her that opportunity.

On my way home from my class, I was talking to Marshall on the phone. As we were talking, he told me to hold on because another call was coming through and it was the hospital. He wasn't on the phone long, maybe less than a minute. However, on my end, the silence in those few seconds allowed me to prepare myself for those words that I wanted to hear—she was finally at peace—and didn't want to hear—that she was gone. The silence was eerie. When he came back on the line, he said, "It was your mother," and I thought, lucky you. He said, "She's gone." I was in a daze and felt like I was having an out-of-body experience. Time seemed to just stop. I have no idea how I was able to drive.

I told him I was five minutes from the hospital and to meet me there. I wouldn't allow my body to shake and quiver. I wouldn't allow my body to explode, to become angry. My thoughts were rampant, this was not supposed to happen to her. She was a good person who didn't deserve the agony of cancer.

My mother never had any consequences for her actions or behaviors. Sometimes the consequences come from a place that is unexpected. Losing a child has to be the most horrible experience any mother, any parent, can go through. This perceived retribution inflicted upon her, unfortunately, was the death of her firstborn child.

The five-minute drive to the hospital felt like forever. I felt like I was still holding on the phone with Marshall when I was on the highway. I arrived at the hospital, parked the car, and sprinted into the building. I did not stop at the front desk for a guest pass; I was done with that. I was running through the corridors and I heard people yelling "*Hey*" at me. I must have bumped into people without even knowing it. I was not focused, not thinking. I didn't have a single thought in my head until I reached the elevator and I couldn't remember the floor she was on. I managed to reach the ICU. I saw my mother sitting in a chair with a blank stare, the only expression was despair. I hugged her, and she held onto me for a few seconds, not minutes, seconds. The only time I actually felt warmth from her arms since I had my ear infection as a young child. I hugged my dad and asked if I could see my sister. I was not afraid to see her body. I didn't touch her as rigor mortis had already set in. I just stood there and stared in disbelief, not knowing what to do next. We stayed in the ICU until they came to remove her body and then they put us in a private room. I told my family I was going down to my car to cancel my appointments.

I got to my car and made some phone calls. One of which was to my cousin who expelled this scream of horror when I told her. When I got out of my car, my car alarm went off, and I couldn't shut it off unless I got back into my car. This was strange, I thought. Again, I got out of my car and the alarm sounded again. I got back in and it stopped. I called the dealership and was instructed on how to shut it off. By this time, I had been in my car for about twenty minutes and was anxious that my husband would be concerned about my absence.

I returned to where my family was, and Dominic was there. My dad said to me, "Diane, I would like to introduce you to your brother," as if I was the one who decided to become estranged from him. I blatantly ignored my dad. Marshall, on the other hand, was concerned about my absence. My Jewish husband firmly said to me, in a voice that expressed dismay, "A priest came in and we had to pray together," and I thought to myself, "So glad my car alarm went off." However, for my Jewish husband, this was much more traumatic. Marshall described the sacred prayerful scene to me. He had to sit between my mother and the "high holy guy," the priest. The priest had suggested that everyone join hands in prayer. Poor Marshall, the little Jewish boy, was sandwiched between the devil and Jesus (my mother and the priest). Afterward he told me he was worried about the possibility of being crucified, concerned that he would burst into flames, as the images of the Last Supper suddenly might have become a reality.

After we left the hospital, we went directly to the funeral home. No one was in any shape to go through picking out a coffin, prayer cards, font size, obituary for the newspaper, nail polish, and hairstyle. This could have been preplanned and saved us from going through this arduous process. When it was all said and done, I told Marshall, we will never do this again and *I will not* put my kids through this. It was worse than the death itself. Therefore, weeks after my sister was buried, my husband and I preplanned our own funeral arrangements.

The day of the wake was the most emotionally exhausting day. The funeral home was packed with about fifty of my brother's "closest friends" and family. I don't think I know fifty people. My parents were like zombies. At the end of the evening, Dominic came up to me and said the following: "I'm sorry for everything I've ever done to you. I want to have a relationship with you." He also apologized to Marshall. I was skeptical. This was grief speaking. This was his need to be the good brother. I accepted his apology and told him reconciliation is a slow process and I'm not going to rush into anything. My sister was buried the next day.

Chapter 32

THE AFTERMATH

I fully understand why, to this day, I have never processed my sister's death. Death was never discussed in my house. I was forbidden to use the "d" word when my sister was battling cancer, and I was forbidden to even discuss her death with my parents after she died. I know my parents grieved, but I never saw them break down. I don't know what it is like to grieve. This explains why I was incapacitated for days and exhausted while writing about this part of my life. I relived every moment of this traumatic process. I always thought I had grieved prior to her leaving us, only to find out that I was absolutely wrong. About a week or two after the funeral, I went to Boston to visit my son at college. During that visit I became exhausted and depressed. At first, I was unable to understand what was going on with myself, and then it hit me. I just lost my sister.

My mother didn't help matters. The very next day right after the funeral, my mother called and said, "If you want anything of your sister's, come now or I'm throwing everything out." She presented it like a fire sale; everything must go *now*, or better yet, as if people were lined up outside her door clamoring to get a dead person's clothes.

When my daughter and I got to the house, what I saw, was unbelievable. How a grieving mother could conjure up such energy was baffling to me. The hospital bed in my sister's room was already taken away. My mother must have had these people on speed dial. I have no idea how she got them to pick up the bed so quickly. Her room was cleaned and sanitized; more sterilized than the operating room where my sister had her surgeries. It was as if cancer was contagious, as if she had COVID. But this was how my mother dealt with anything that was too emotional. She erased it from her mind. She hit the delete button, to make as if it never existed. But as we all know nothing is ever permanently deleted. Memories cannot be deleted. They stay on our hard drive. I truly expected one or both of my parents to die of a broken heart shortly after my sister's death. However, they lived for another ten years after her death.

My daughter took my sister's computer desk and maybe some of her bracelets, not quite sure. I also took some of her bangle bracelets. However, my mother would not give them to me unless I promised I would wear them. So, I lied and told her I would wear them. I just wanted the bracelets to remember her by. Unfortunately, as is usually the case, the memory of the deceased seems to become less apparent and begins to fade. That disturbed me to the point of eventually getting inked, putting the breast cancer ribbon on my forearm, along with her name and the date of her death. I did not want her memory to fade.

My father, on the other hand, was clearly grieving. He said, "I lost my best friend," a clear indication of where my mother ranked in his life. My dad was in mourning. He would sit in his chair, staring at nothing, and being very quiet and despondent at times. But there was also no discussion with him either. I do remember my dad saying to me that my brother was "his rock," probably because Dominic would tell him what he wanted to hear. But I am not that person who can do that. I am a realist and unable to sugarcoat anything. I always thought my bluntness and honesty were negative traits until one day I read something, somewhere, stating the following: "People who are honest and blunt can always be trusted. You will never have to guess or question where they are coming from and what their motives are because there will not be any underlying, hidden agenda; nothing will be hidden."

After about a week, my mother started talking about the ICU nurse and how terribly the nurse treated my sister. I told my mother she *must* write a letter to the top administrator of the hospital, as I would do the same. I put my social work cap on, did my research, and gave my mother the information as to where and to whom to send the letter. We collaborated on what to write and sent out the letters. About a few days to a week later, I received a phone call from an administrator. I told her how unprofessional the nurse was. My sister was terrified of dying. The day she died, she was vomiting and unable to breathe, so she kept ringing for her ICU nurse to help alleviate her discomfort. As I previously mentioned, the ICU nurse complained to me about my sister "bothering" her all morning. It was unfortunate that on her last day of life, she had to deal with a nurse who had no compassion.

When I wrote the letter, I did not mention that my sister actually had passed under this nurse's care. The administrator didn't quite pick up on the nuances of our conversation, that she had passed, and not putting it in the letter was deliberate. The administrator asked me how my sister was doing and I told her she had passed on that day in the ICU. The administrator gasped and was clearly disturbed by the entire incident and told me that this was not the first time she had heard complaints about this nurse, following up with "This will be the last time she does this here; it will be taken care of." I assume the nurse was fired. My experience working in a hospital has taught me how to manage the administrative red tape and expedite appropriate treatment for a patient, even if it is for yourself.

I made myself available to my parents, as much as possible. Their negative treatment toward me had somewhat decreased for a bit, and I was powerless, unable to turn my back on them. The grief, sadness, and loss were something I had never experienced before. The emotional roller coaster I was on for the two years my sister was fighting this disease was the ebb and flow of the ocean, except this ocean ebbed for the last time and all that was left was the graininess, the granularity of dry sand. I was in the Sahara Desert, feeling parched, thirsty for an explanation, an understanding as to why this happened, left with just questions and no answers. I was left with the vast expanse of emptiness within a desert of despair. The sadness of the sand encroached into every crevice of my being. I was bereft.

The absence of neglect, ridicule, and disappointment was short-lived. The family of four was always a family of four and not five. At the time of my sister's death, Dominic decided to accompany my parents to the cemetery to pick out the plot where my sister would be buried. I had no issue with that. What I came to find out later, of course, without anyone speaking to me prior to making the decision, was my parents and my brother decided to get a "family" plot for only the four of them, my parents, my brother, and my sister. I truthfully never wanted to be buried with them, as I had too much difficulty living with them. However, it continues to validate my sense of not belonging and feeling left out—overlooked and forgotten again. They never conferred with me about the plot.

As a clinician, I had always suggested to my clients to journal, to help them with their feelings, and to give themselves a voice. It is irrelevant if there is nobody in the room to hear you. You can hear *you*. The important thing is giving a voice to yourself. I have never journaled. However, writing this piece about my sister has enabled me to process her death and allowed me to grieve in a way that was not possible for me to do years before. It helped me to release emotions that were buried so deep inside of me that I was unable to stick my hand into the vat of wretchedness and allow myself to release the vermin of grief to escape. I have now been able to finally expel the sadness and grief, which I have held inside of me for all these years. However, every now and then, her death continues to touch my heart and I break down.

Chapter 33

LIFE GOES ON

I called my parents almost every day. It didn't bother me to do that because we were all in pain, and on some level, I could not imagine how my parents felt about losing a child. Even though I never lost a child, I was able to empathize with them, and I didn't have the heart to abandon them. Grieving can only be described as a "bipolar" experience, with periods of feeling really good and other times of feeling really bad. But that eventually passed, and life became normalized again.

My parents aged rapidly after my sister died and required more care. My father was not driving anymore, as his memory started to fail prior to my sister's passing. My mother, on the other hand, resented having to do more than her share. For example, she now had to do all of the driving that my dad used to do. She eventually rebelled and relied on me to drive her places, primarily her doctor appointments. What that meant was on my days off from work, I would spend most of my time in the doctor's office with her.

About a mile away from their house, a fifty-five-and-older community condo was being built. Dominic and I both urged them to take advantage of moving before things got really bad. They were already having difficulty with the stairs in their house. The location of this condo was convenient because they had lived in the same town for several decades and they knew where everything was. They did not have to acclimate to new surroundings.

They sold their house with the help of my cousin who was a real estate agent. Marshall and I helped them pack and get rid of stuff they no longer needed; after fifty years in the same house, there was a lot of stuff. We went there a couple of times a week to help them sort out what should be kept and what should be thrown out. I am not sure if Dominic helped them pack, but it was all very strange. Even with as much resentment as I had toward my mother, I had this "human" feeling that made it possible for me to be there for both of them without feeling angry. Marshall and I even paid for "Got Junk" to pick up the crap they were throwing out. I did that because they always complained about not having enough money, and I was financially able to do that for them. It was not until much later that I found out why they were so concerned about money.

They closed on their house and had to move out before their condo was completed and ready to be moved into. My brother decided to take them in. I had said to Dominic that I was surprised he was taking them in considering he had just as many complaints about them as I did. He said, "Dad has been very good to me." I said, "Really, how so?" I was incapable of realizing what exactly he was talking about, but his hesitation was a clue his life was not going well and a clue I should have tapped into. Dominic said,

"Well, Dad helped me when we (he and his new wife) moved into our new house." I asked, "How did he help you?" He said, "He bought us a washer and dryer." I said, "Wow, I got nothing when I moved into my house." My parents put their belongings in storage and they moved in with my brother.

Once their house was sold, I had told my dad not to put the money he got from the house in a bank that was paying very little interest. I told him to invest it in a high-interest account that he would be able to withdraw from at a moment's notice. He told me he did exactly what I said. Hearing that from him gave me a sense of importance. I felt appreciated.

But staying at my brother's house was not good for my parents nor Dominic. My brother had just as much trouble with them as I did. He was unable to handle being with them all the time and would take off on weekends to get away from them. What that meant was my parents would call me to come get them and spend a day with me. Ironically, when they were at our house, my dad would tell me how wonderful it was to be in my house. He said it was calming and quiet.

Dominic complained frequently about them, and my parents complained about him and his wife. It was a shit show. But the day came when their condo was finished and they moved into their new place. Everyone was relieved, especially my parents, as change was not something they accepted gracefully, especially at their age. This feeling of displacement made my mother feel out of control.

As time went on, my brother and I started to collaborate more on how to manage my parents. During the week when my brother and I were both at work, they would call both me and my brother continuously, all day long. I had four phone numbers, my home number, my cell, my home office number, and my actual office number. They would first call Dominic, then call all four of my other numbers until they reached one of us.

As an example, my father called me one day, left a message, and said I had to call him immediately and that it was urgent. I had had back-to-back clients that day and called him at nine at night when I got out of work. When I called him and told him I had just gotten out of work, instead of discussing the reason for his call, he proceeded to talk about why I worked so late. He said: "Why do you work so late? It's not safe for you to come home in the dark alone. Aren't you tired?" His questions didn't upset me too much, as he was not accusatory, controlling, or punitive, but sounded more inquisitive and concerned than anything else. When I asked him what had happened during the day that he needed to speak to me about, he said he didn't know.

Chapter 34

THE MEETING OF THE MINDS

The more my parents required assistance, the closer my brother and I came together. We were a united force. My parents wanted me and my brother to quit our jobs and be their full-time caregivers. I truly believe they wanted *me* to quit my job and care for them and not necessarily have my brother care for them.

We first gave my parents an option to have someone come in to care for them, and my mother was adamantly against it. She wanted me to care for them and not some stranger. It was difficult enough for her to have a nurse come in and care for my sister when my sister was sick; she was not going to have someone take care of her who was not family. I believe it was also more psychological than anything else. If someone had to come in to take care of them, for my mother, that would have been an indication that their health was declining and they had begun to deteriorate. This would have been impossible for my mother to acknowledge. Obviously, that would also mean my mother would have to give up control to someone else, something she just could not tolerate. Also on some level, if I was her caretaker, she could continue to control me.

Therefore, after we did some research into assisted living facilities, we decided to have a sit-down with my parents and try to encourage them to at least visit a place. My mother declined to look at a place. My father, however, was open to seeing what it was like. Since my dad had a more positive outlook on this, my mother's vote was vetoed.

My brother immediately set up an appointment to look at a facility. This was the same facility my dad's sister was in, and it was about forty-five minutes from our houses. The facility was privately owned and was not the usual facility most people would think of. It was a big old house with a small number of residents living there, probably fifteen to twenty people. For me, I felt my parents would get more individual attention, which was positive. Most of the rooms were on the second floor and there were a few rooms on the first floor. But they had a stair lift to transport residents who had difficulty climbing stairs. My mother refused to use the stair lift because she was vain and was unable to accept her own aging process. In the dining room, they had a professional chef cooking for the residents and a nice-sized TV in the living room. They had all the activities available to them like a much bigger facility would have.

My dad was all for it. In his words, "Sign me up." My mother said no way, but, then again, my father vetoed her vote. My mom was not budging, and I basically said, "If you don't move, I will not be helping you anymore. I cannot do it. I work. I have a business to run. I'm not capable of caring for you in addition to working" (nor did I want to). The decision was made, and they were going to assisted living within three weeks. Now we had to convince my dad to sign over all his finances to me, and we had to obtain an attorney to change the will and hand over power of attorney to whomever my parents decided to give that power.

On the ride home from the facility, my mother was like a caged animal. She was *not* going! I talked to my father about putting me in charge of all his financial accounts. He couldn't put Dominic's name on any of his accounts as Dominic had filed for bankruptcy and the creditors would take all of my parents' money. We arrived at the condo and my father gathered up all his financial information. The three of us—me, Dad, and Marshall—drove to every bank he had money in and he added my name to all of his accounts. There was only one bank that my mother needed to be present for, so we drove back to the condo and picked her up. My mother looked worse than the day my sister died. My dad was as happy as a puppy with his tongue hanging out and his tail wagging, being placed in a new home full of love, fun, and attention.

When we got back to their condo, I was handed all the bank books and all the information I needed to manage their money. His checkbook was like an episode of *Everybody Loves Raymond* when Debra handed over the finances to Ray. In that episode, Ray had several checkbooks with different entries and nothing balanced, while bouncing several checks. I was unable to figure out what my dad did, as he wrote checks without documenting anything. When he did document as having made a payment, there was no corroboration of payment based on the bank statements he had received. It took me days to come within dollars of balancing the checkbook to the bank statement. For someone who doesn't do math, I *am* able to balance a checkbook.

I was happy that I was the one who was managing my parents' money, primarily because "I knew how to manage money." However, I also knew I might be under tremendous scrutiny. I didn't want to be accused by Dominic or my parents of stealing their money. I, therefore, kept a ledger documenting everything that came into the bank and everything that went out, right down to the socks and underwear that were purchased. I had to be squeaky clean.

We set up a meeting with the attorney whom my husband and I had used for our wills. We did this so we could set up health care proxies and powers of attorney. Little did I expect the topsoil of the ground to shake, crack, and try to suck me into the crust, the gravel of the earth. Remember Dominic's hesitation when I asked him what my father had done for him that he needed to metamorphically "repay" him. Dominic emailed me about a week prior to the appointment with the attorney. He told me he had "borrowed" a great deal of money from my dad, probably about a third of my parents' life savings. He told me this because all of this was going to become public at the attorney's office. I was shaking as if an electrical charge, a lightning bolt, was penetrating my body, and I was going to combust and be reduced to ashes. I realized that my father's emotional state at the time of that "loan" was such that he was in no condition to make that kind of financial decision and lend my brother *that* amount of money. My dad had been taken advantage of by my brother, his son, as I knew Dominic would never pay him back—and he didn't.

We met with the lawyer. My parents met with the attorney first and then we (Marshall, Dominic, and me) joined them later on. The most fascinating thing was the following. When the attorney asked my parents whom they wanted as their health care proxy, surprisingly, they said, "Diane," not Dominic. Dominic was made second in command. Another shock wave pierced through my body. But I was up for the job, and they would do well by me. I also had my husband to educate me on medical issues if I needed help understanding certain medical terms. Aside from all this, the condo was put in my name only.

Arrangements were made with a moving company to move a couple of pieces of furniture to the assisted living facility. I made those arrangements and told the movers they were *only* to take orders from me and no one else. I knew my mother would call them the day before to cancel their services. I also told the movers that this would happen, and if my mom did call, they would have to call me immediately. The day before they left the condo to move into assisted living, my mother called the movers to cancel! The movers called me immediately to confirm whether to cancel or go ahead with the move. I told them to go ahead with the move.

Prior to moving, I asked my parents how much they wanted to be involved with their own funeral arrangements, coffins, etc. They wanted to have some control, so they agreed to prearrange their funeral. Prior to dropping them off at assisted living, we made a stop at the funeral home. All the arrangements were made and off we went to their new home. After we dropped them off, we met up with Dominic at a mall. I had decided that it would be a good idea for my brother to live in my parents' condo since he was looking for a new place and it was a way to avoid spending all their money. My brother paid for all the utilities and taxes on the condo, which was still cheaper than any other place he would be living in. As we entered the parking lot of the mall, Dominic was waiting for us outside his car. As we approached, he did a cartwheel in the parking lot. I think that says it all.

Chapter 35

THE ADJUSTMENT

Change is not always a bad thing, especially if you are in control of that change. For the elderly, change is not always something they can control. My mother never adjusted to living in a place that was not her home. Alzheimer's has hit almost every one of my family members as they aged. Obviously, learning from experience is not something that my family entertains, as one could eat healthily and exercise to at least delay the onset. My parents ate terribly as long as I have been around. They never wanted to change their eating habits or change anything about themselves. No one grows up saying, "Can't wait till I'm old so I can go into assisted living or a nursing home." However, there are ways to prevent oneself from going into such a facility. My parents could have put the money they gave Dominic toward purchasing long-term care insurance. That insurance could have enabled them to have someone come into their home and care for them, even though that was not what they would have wanted. That way, there would have been no burden on the children and my parents would not have had to leave their familiar surroundings. Adjusting to new surroundings puts stress on the person and speeds up the effects of dementia.

I learned a great deal from my parents' mistakes. My funeral arrangements are done. I was fortunate enough to obtain long-term care insurance that will allow me to stay at home when I totally lose my mind and not burden my children. Additionally, I go to the gym three times a week and work out with a personal trainer who has taught me how to eat healthier and avoid processed foods. I have been doing this for nearly twelve years now. Given how I grew up and my addiction to junk food, it doesn't always work. However, I am able to maintain a healthy body weight most of the time. Even though I may be doomed and may not be able to escape Alzheimer's, I'm trying to delay the process as much as possible.

As for my husband, he does not have long-term care insurance. He has longevity. His mother passed when she was ninety-one and his father passed when he was ninety-eight. His uncle passed when he was ninety-nine. None of these people passed from Alzheimer's but from other medical issues. I always tell my husband, "If the Nazis didn't get you, you will live forever" (his family were Holocaust survivors).

The first few months my parents were in assisted living, my mother would call several times a day to "get me out of here." We finally had to remove the phone from their room and cut off access. I would visit them weekly, and eventually the interval between visits extended to two weeks, three weeks, and then it stopped altogether.

I have a good understanding of Alzheimer's. I did my first internship working with the elderly on an inpatient unit. My dad made a comment to me one day, which I am sure was due to his dementia. However, when he said what he said, I had a visceral reaction. This was said in private. My father told me "he knew" I was stealing his money. Suddenly, I felt like I was in a room in which everyone was dressed in Victorian garb. Men with their top hats and women with their petticoats, bustles, and full skirts, dancing the Viennese waltz. The music stopped, and everyone was staring at me emotionally blunted, faces restricted, constricted, gawking at me. I felt the grenade perforate my body, puncturing every organ that was left inside of me. There was nothing left of me. I was a shell of myself, a skeleton. I looked at my father and said, "I'm never coming back here, I will never see you again." And that was the last time I saw them alive.

Now, I suppose most of you are thinking, "Most elderly accuse their family members of stealing their money," and that is correct. It probably was the Alzheimer's speaking. But this was a big trigger for me because it was my brother who actually took money from him and the history of me being blamed for everything.

My parents stayed in assisted living for a couple of years and were eventually forced to leave. They required a level of care that the assisted living facility was unable to give. The assisted living director told my brother and me that we had two weeks to get them out. This was definitely not on our agenda. Since I was their main health care proxy and continued to maintain their medical care, I felt the responsibility was on me. However, Dominic did his part.

Two weeks! I knew assisted living could not throw them out on the street. However, Dominic and I were not equipped to have them live with us. I, therefore, did what I normally do when I need guidance. I called June. June worked in nursing homes and would be able to guide me to the appropriate place—and she did. She gave me the name and phone number of the administrator of the nursing home she worked at. Bingo! They had a room for a married couple that was available immediately. This was a miracle for us. Within the week, we had the assisted living facility move them to the nursing home.

Chapter 36

HOW I BECAME FREE FROM THE CONSTANT ANXIETY

My mother frequented the ER during her stay in the nursing home, and most of my time I spent on the phone talking to medical personnel. My mother was not sick with cancer or diabetes or anything like that. Most of her hospitalizations pertained to aging. It was January 2016 and I remember my husband and I were walking on the boardwalk. How do I remember this? Well, I don't like exercising, especially in the cold. With that being said, I received a phone call from the hospital stating she was admitted and they asked if she had a DNR and/or a living will. I honestly don't know what goes on with assisted living and nursing homes, as every time my mother is admitted into the hospital, I receive the same phone call. These documents, as I was told, should have accompanied my mother when admitted to the hospital.

I remember the day being icy cold and I can see the snow clouds forming, the blue-gray clouds that completely cover the sky. The forecast predicted a big snowstorm, several inches for the following day. Since I love snow, I always remember snowstorms. I said to my husband, I will drive in a blizzard to get these documents to the hospital if I have to. My mother was ninety-one and she had no quality of life; therefore, there was no reason to prolong her life. It turned out the hospital did have the papers it needed.

The following day, I received a call from the hospital informing me that my mother had pneumonia. I turned to my husband and said, "She will be gone within two days." Exactly, two days later, when I was in my office, I received a phone call from the hospital asking, again, if there was a DNR and living will. I said yes. They told me her heart stopped. I thought back to when Dominic said to the doctor who wanted to put a pacemaker in her, "She has a heart?" The nurse said they were resuscitating her. Without realizing it, I went ballistic, yelling, "Don't resuscitate, she has a DNR!" The nurse, I believe, stopped the procedure. In the meantime, they had called my brother to tell him she was gone. I finally reached my brother, and he said the hospital told him she was gone. I had to make sure she was dead and called the hospital back. They confirmed she had passed.

And then there are times when being married to Marshall is like being married to the Keystone Cops. I called Marshall to tell him my mother passed. He was always concerned about how I would react to her passing because none of the issues I had with her were ever resolved.

I called him up. He answered. I said to him, "Guess who died?" He says, "Abe Vigoda." I did *not* expect that answer. Again, I said, "Guess who died?" And again, he said, "Abe Vigoda." Well, after several times going back and forth and his response always being the same, I decided to throw in the towel and said to him, "My mother." I believe he was more upset about Abe Vigoda. Abe Vigoda was the walking dead on the *Barney Miller* TV sitcom for years.

I stayed at work seeing clients until nine at night with no creeping thoughts about my mother's passing. It was a relief because I thought she was going to live forever. The poison was flushed out of my body, the way someone would pop a pimple, the pus comes shooting out and is gone in an instant. I felt my complexion clear up. I felt clean with clear thoughts. The anxiety that had imprisoned me all of my life had just been pardoned with no probation to restrain me. I had experienced my anxiety as a life sentence without the possibility of parole. However, the death of my mother, metaphorically, unlocked the ankle bracelets that I had worn since childhood. I was finally acquitted. I was free.

As I drove home at the end of my workday, I tried to contemplate how I would enter the apartment and greet my husband. There were no tears, no regrets, no sadness. I took better care of my parents than they did of me. I did the human thing to make sure they were cared for. As I opened the door to my unit, Marshall jumped up from the couch, approached me as he widened his arms to hug me. He was approaching me with the offering of empathetic comfort with his embrace. Unfortunately for him, this obviously stimulated an Irish jig on my part. I, spontaneously, went into a dance, shuffling my feet and waving my arms into the air. He stood there dumbfounded by my exuberance, as I danced with an air of freedom. For the first time in my life, I was able to exhale, allowing all the toxins to be expelled from my body (of course at that point I had to open all the windows to refresh the room, as I didn't want the toxins to permeate the atmosphere anymore). The chains were removed, and I was finally released from captivity.

Chapter 37

THE FUNERAL

The following day the three of us (my husband, Dominic, and me) went to the funeral home to set up the viewing, as the arrangements had been previously made. A few years back I had made a decision to prepay their funeral expenses with their money because I was concerned there would be no money left at the time of their death, and I was not going to be responsible for the entire funeral bill.

That afternoon, I received a phone call from the priest who was going to perform the funeral service. He had asked me a question for which he didn't expect the answer I gave him. I suspect he might have been new on the job because the silence I heard in response to my answer was noteworthy. The priest was muted, reticent. I, figuratively, surgically removed his tongue with the answer I gave him, making him speechless. It seemed as if it was the first time anyone ever gave him that answer. The priest had asked me to tell him something about my mother. I did not expect to even have a conversation with a priest, as it never entered my mind. My bluntness, impulsiveness, and honesty just poured out. I responded to him by saying: "I have nothing nice to say about my mother as she was not a good mother to me. If you want some positive feedback about her, I will give you my brother's phone number and you can talk to him." He kindly and hesitantly said, "Um, no thank you," and hung up the phone. I suspect it was his first day on the job because he never called my brother.

I have always had a difficult time when a less-than-honorable person dies and they are praised as if they were Jesus Christ. It honestly turns my stomach. I also believe I would not be able to live with myself if I felt forced to praise someone who treated me with such disdain. Sometimes in life we have to suck it up and do things because "it's the right thing to do." However, I could not bring myself to praise someone who made it very clear to me that I was unwanted and made me feel unlovable.

Prior to the wake, I told Dominic that I needed to be alone with Mom as she lay in her coffin, before anyone came into the room. He agreed. I told my husband to come with me. He had no idea what would transpire, but I wanted him to be a witness to what I was about to say to her. I stood there looking down at her dead body knowing I would have the last words. I said to her, "It didn't have to be this way, you didn't have to treat me this way, you could have changed. Fuck you." My husband stood there, frozen in place, feet nailed to the floor. He was breathless and astounded. His eyes looked almost piercing, as I thought that nails were going to shoot out from his eyes and strike me in my jugular vein. He wasn't angry with me, just shocked that I had said that. He understood where I was coming from. He stood there and asked me if I was OK. I said, "I'm perfect."

I never shed a tear for my mother's passing, and I had no regrets about anything. My job as an adult child was to make sure both my parents were safe from harm and well taken care of and I did exactly that. There is no law that an adult child has to visit their parents. I made appropriate medical decisions for both of them. But there was no love lost. Most would think "How could you be like that?" But most likely those people have good parents who showed them love and support. That was not my experience.

Chapter 38

THE DEATH OF MY FATHER

During a conversation we had with the funeral home, Dominic and I mentioned that my father would pass soon after my mother, as we knew he would not survive long after she died. My mother died on January 25 and my father passed on February 26 of that same year. One month after my mother. My father never knew my mother died, as his Alzheimer's had gotten the better of him. However, I believe my father was not going to precede her in death because he knew how difficult it would have been for her, regardless of whether or not she had all her faculties. I also believe that my dad needed a month of peace before he joined her in the grave.

I was notified by the hospital that he had passed. Days before, we had been informed that he was slipping away. I called Dominic, who was clearly upset by the news. I, too, was upset but only became emotional when I told my kids. I had more compassion for my dad, as I always saw him as a reasonable person.

Given it had been only a month since we planned my mom's funeral, everything was fresh in our heads, and we knew exactly what we had to do. This time I didn't get a call from the priest. I guess he felt he wasn't going to go down that road again. My husband and I went to the florist. We walked in and said to the florist, "Remember us?" She said, "Yes." I said we need the same floral arrangements as last month, just change everything from mother and grandmother to father and grandfather.

I eulogized my father, which I didn't do for my mother. As seldom as he interacted with me, he did have a positive impact on me. In a subtle way, he made me the independent person I am today, something he was unable to do with my siblings. I do miss him and occasionally think about him.

However, that does not mean there wasn't any drama at the funeral. When my parents left their condo and needed supervised care, I eventually took all my mother's jewelry because my brother and I did not want anyone stealing her engagement and wedding rings. I asked him if I could keep them. I wanted to eventually take the diamonds and make up necklaces for my four granddaughters when they turned sixteen. Dominic was fine with that. Dominic, however, never discussed with me what he was going to do with my dad's military mementos. He unilaterally made a decision to give the military memorabilia to his son because his son was in the military. He did this without discussing it with me first. My son had been interested in some of my dad's army keepsakes.

Without my knowledge, my kids went back to the funeral home and got the American flag that was presented to me at the burial site even though Dominic wanted it. Dominic was very upset when he found out my kids took the flag. At that time, I knew nothing of this until Dominic called me and I told him he needed to call my son. Eventually they came to some sort of agreement. Although the flag remains with my kids.

Chapter 39

THE UNANTICIPATED HEARTACHE

Two thousand sixteen was a year of several unanticipated funerals. The actual number of deaths escapes my memory; I think around ten to twelve people that we knew passed or had family members pass. That year, there was only one funeral though that deeply touched me, and was for someone whom I still grieve for today.

For a while, June and I weren't in close communication, primarily because life got in the way. We spoke on the phone and got together for dinner but not too often. Two of her daughters lived out of state and she would visit them frequently, as she missed seeing her grandkids. I was busy working a lot and also spending time with my own grandkids. I believe at this point June had retired from her job and she and her husband were doing a lot of traveling.

One day while we were speaking on the phone, she had told me that Jim, her husband, wasn't doing well, and the doctors were not sure what was going on with him. I believe it was at that point when we started to speak to each other more frequently, as both Marshall and I were concerned about him. Unfortunately, Jim had gone undiagnosed and misdiagnosed for a long time, and eventually, he was diagnosed with esophageal cancer.

I remembered thinking to myself: "How often should I call her? Is once a week too much? Is every two weeks too long of a time span?" When someone has a serious medical issue, the caregiver usually is the "go-to" person to find out how the person is doing. However, the caregiver usually spends hours talking to friends and family, repeating the same story over and over again, in addition to caring for the loved one. It is exhausting! And when someone has cancer, there are many hospitalizations. But I wanted June to know I was there for her whenever she wanted to talk.

During the spring of that year, he was hospitalized frequently, and June was right by his side. She slept in the hospital room with him during every hospital stay. Marshall and I visited him once when he was in the hospital, as I knew he wasn't going to live much longer. I am not sure June knew he had so little time left. Marshall had told me he wanted to have a private conversation with him about the end of his life. I left the room with June, and we sat in a waiting room down the hall, just talking. Marshall told me they had a forthright discussion about Jim's impending demise. He validated all of Jim's concerns, and they embraced for a long and final hug.

I believe it was a matter of a few weeks when Jim was hospitalized again. He was put in hospice, and I asked June if we could come and visit. Her kids were there and I knew it was going to be any day. June gave us the OK to come up to the hospital. We were maybe twenty minutes from home when I got a text from June telling us not to come and that she would call me later. I knew what that meant, and I had hoped we would see him for the last time, but it was too late.

I could not imagine what she was going through or how she would manage to get through this painful time. I told myself I needed to be there for her the way she was there for me when I needed her. Her children took very good care of her just as she took very good care of her kids when they were young. My heart broke for her, as she lost her best friend and she was alone in her house.

To this day, the rules for helping someone through the grieving process are quite foreign to me. I have never observed anyone who was emotionally healthy enough to show me how to handle a situation like this. I wanted to be supportive of June but wasn't sure how to do it, especially since we were about an hour away from each other. Even though I feel I failed her in some way, I would call her every week on the days I got home early from work. I would drive up to have lunch with her and sometimes dinner. But June was doing all the right things. She got out of the house daily and had a close network of friends close to where she lived. She had a good support system and her youngest daughter lived close by. She spent a lot of time there with her grandkids.

The hardest thing for me, and it in no way compares to June's pain, was not being able to express to her how I felt about Jim's death. I was afraid of upsetting her, and, again, it doesn't compare to her loss. I still keep it bottled up inside of me.

And then COVID hit and no one was going anywhere. We stayed away from each other for about a year and a half but continued to talk on the phone. I believe it was the summer of 2021 when June said she, her daughter, and the grandkids were coming to Long Branch to go to Seven Presidents beach. I told her to come to my house because she wouldn't have to pay for parking, and they would have the convenience of my house to shower and clean up before they went home. She spoke to her daughter, and they agreed to come to my house.

June called from the parking lot to tell me they had arrived. I ran down the stairs to meet her. I believe I flew down the stairs, as I don't remember my feet ever touching the ground. I felt my heart pounding with excitement, as I had missed her so much. We spotted each other, nearly running—well, walking fast cause neither of us can run anymore—and hugged each other. We held onto each other as if it would be the last time we would see each other. Our eyes filled with water. Our arms embracing each other, neither of us letting go. It was such an emotional moment for both of us because, like everyone else, we were isolated for so long because of COVID. We had a wonderful day at the beach, as that summer was very rainy. But this day was a bright, sunny day with low humidity. Her grandchildren were delightful and had a great time playing in the sand and running in the ocean. It was wonderful to reconnect with her.

I never asked June if she was interested in dating. I felt it was inappropriate and had no idea where she was at with respect to her grieving. But one morning as I was walking into my office, she texted me a picture of herself with a guy. My hand froze and I was unable to move my fingers fast enough to find her in my contact list. Speed dial appeared not to be fast enough for me, either, at that moment. She started dating this man who has the same interests as she does. I am so happy for her. She is no longer alone. She has a companion. I'm beyond thrilled. I am so happy I could fart. Coincidentally, he has the same name as her late husband…Jim! We, therefore, have a part of Jim with us now every time we see June and "new" Jim.

Maybe someday I will learn to grieve in a way that will allow me to process a loss when it happens and not years later. I miss Jim and I miss my sister, but I still have a long way to go to process their deaths.

Chapter 40

PERSEVERANCE

The year my parents died, my brother left the country and moved to Ecuador with his wife. We never had the opportunity to say goodbye because he was busy saying goodbye to all of his "friends." The feeling of desertion and abandonment flooded my body once more. My childhood feelings of being alienated overwhelmed me, as the silence of loneliness was emphasized by the desolate condition I felt he left me in. My entire family was now absent in the here and now. But just as in the past, the sense of alienation at that moment was devastating me.

Everyone has the right to make their own decisions and to do what makes them happy. I don't fault him for wanting to leave the country. However, before he left the country, I pleaded with him for us to get together, as I knew it would probably be the last time I would see him. The last time I spoke to him he said to me, "We are busy packing up and are unable to have dinner with you." Yet I kept seeing him out to dinner with friends on Facebook. I never received a phone call from him before he left.

I had to reframe my thoughts and not allow my anger to consume me. In my heart I always knew who I could trust.

Diane Harth

There was always evidence and validation that it wasn't my brother; it was my husband, my children, and June. They were the people who never failed me and the ones I could always count on.

As previously stated, my relationship with my brother would permanently end, as I was never going to be the ATM that my father was for him. We always hear people say, "But it's family, and you can't turn your back on family." Except my family not only could but did turn their backs on me repeatedly. We also can't enable one's poor behavior. There comes a time when people have to take responsibility for their own behavior and "become an adult." My family was toxic for me, and they were not sufficiently supportive of my mental health. Since my biological family has no longer been in my life, I have less stress and fewer doubts about myself as a person, and live a much happier and healthier emotional life. My life is more enriched by the people with whom I choose to connect.

There was one last incident in which Dominic made it very easy for me to completely sever the relationship. About a year after my parents died, I received a letter from their insurance company indicating that I had overpaid their premium. This happened at the time when Dominic and I were applying to Medicaid for them. I had told the insurance company that they had passed and the company told me it needed both me and Dominic to sign a document to release funds. I emailed Dominic and asked him to make me primary executor and relinquish his rights. He agreed. However, he said it would cost a few hundred dollars for him to receive and send the documents back to me because the government in Ecuador can confiscate the mail. Therefore, the documents had to be sent in a way that would bypass the regular mail, using something comparable to FedEx, which would be more costly. He wanted me to Venmo the money to him in order to do this. I thought to myself that considering all the money he took from my parents, why couldn't he afford a few hundred dollars? With all the Facebook photos of him going out to dinner every night, I was sure he was able to afford this. I decided I wasn't going to pay him. That was the last time I had any communication with him. The insurance company worked with me and I was able to get the refund. As an aside, in my parents' will, it stated that I would receive any money that might be reimbursed to their estate, up to the point at which it reached half the amount that Dominic had "borrowed" from my parents.

It has been years since I have spoken to Dominic. I don't miss him, but I do think about him every so often. He's still my brother. My cousin Dennis hears from him, and I occasionally ask Dennis how he's doing, just to make sure he's OK.

As long as my family was present in my life, I continued to look for acceptance and love from them. Now that they no longer existed, I was free. I was no longer lonely. My focus was on those who made me feel good about who I am and those who accepted me unconditionally. I focused on cultivating friendships and recognizing that relationships are something that do not happen overnight. Trusting and getting to know someone takes a long time, and in the past, patience was never one of my strong suits. I learned to have patience from my husband who, basically, has *too* much patience. However, many of his good traits have rubbed off on me.

Chapter 41

THE PARALLEL UNIVERSE

With all of my psychotherapy and psychoanalysis, I continued to vacillate between listening to the archaic voices in my head (my mother) and the reframed voices in my ears telling me I am a good person. For most of my life, I heard nothing but criticism and negativity, not only from my mother but also from my ex and his family.

My husband and I are now living full-time in our condo at the beach. This is a new experience and a good experience for many reasons. Living at the beach gives us a sense of calmness and serenity. Listening to the waves crash along the shoreline. The seagulls swoop overhead calling out huoh-huoh-huoh. You close your eyes and you feel the sun penetrating through your skin, warming your body, the way a mother would cradle her baby. The ebb and flow of the ocean is like being in a state of suspended animation, not having a care in the world. There is no distress.

But one particular benefit of living on the beach was that Marshall and I began to have a social life. This social life made us more whole, not only as a couple but as independent people too. It was the necessary piece of the puzzle that was missing when we lived up north. Living in a condo forces you to interact with others—which has its pros and cons. One can be surrounded by people you don't like or may be difficult to be around, along with being surrounded by people you feel more comfortable with. Once we moved to the beach permanently, we became very good friends with the contractor who renovated our unit and also the real estate agent who sold us the place. In addition, I started to go to a personal trainer and about a year later my husband started to train with him. This also turned into a friendship and a way of socializing more, along with staying fit and learning how to eat healthily. We see Scott, our trainer, three times a week, more than we see anyone else.

The more people we met and the more we socialized with our new friends, the more confident I felt about myself and the less the negative thoughts seeped into my consciousness. I was less tormented by the old tape running through my head. I heard less and less of my mother's voice saying, "Why did you do this, why did you say that, you're embarrassing me, you can't do that." The emotional disease in my head had been removed and a transformation has taken place. I had a "momectomy." I felt good about myself and who I was, and I was learning how to depend on others a little more, instead of feeling like I had to do everything on my own. The words of Dr. D reentered my brain: "No man is an island." I learned to trust others and the brick wall that surrounded my being, my soul, was slowly becoming dismantled, one brick at a time. My life was becoming my own, and I felt all of the worry, concern, and apprehension that encapsulated my entire life leave me. The roots of a tree that wrapped around my core, my being, slowly strangulating me, creating the cracks in my personality and self-esteem, these emotions, the aura, left my body, removing all the bad karma that had previously entangled me. The vulture that had followed me, was now a hummingbird injecting these positive sensations into my body, allowing me to be peaceful. My home was now by the ocean and has become my sanctuary.

Because of and in spite of my mother, I became the resilient, strong person I am today. I was the only person I could rely on and trust. Of course, as a child, this was all unconscious and I was not aware of this until much later in life. This is my parallel universe. I also believe I inherited my strength and resilience from my paternal grandmother and great-grandmother. They were both tough and would not take crap from anyone. My father was even afraid of them.

I had to fight and struggle for everything, not only what I wanted but what I needed in my life. I received the basic needs of food, clothing, and shelter from my parents, but my emotional well-being came from my own resources and relying on myself. If I had listened to my parents, I still would have been in a bad first marriage, would not have become educated, and surely never would have had the opportunity to start my own practice. By having the courage and strength to care for myself and be "selfish," especially divorcing the father of my children, I was able to grow out of that sheltered, gender-specific household I grew up in and become the successful therapist that I had hoped to be. I stopped listening to my parents, who thought they knew what was best for me. What I learned from this was to encourage my kids to do what they wanted to do, even if I thought they were possibly not making the right choices. I am not sure that parents always know what is right for their kids. As painful as it is at times, parents have to allow their kids to find their own way.

Chapter 42

HOW MANY THERAPISTS DOES IT TAKE TO CHANGE A LIGHT BULB? ZERO. THE LIGHT BULB CHANGES ONLY IF IT WANTS TO CHANGE.

Change takes a lot of time. It is not something that happens overnight, and it only happens if someone has the desire and the motivation to change. Due to therapy, I changed things that were not in my awareness, that I had no idea needed changing. Behavioral traits are not always genetic, they are also learned. My mother was self-centered and unable to be empathic. She had no filter and would say things without thinking. I had those traits too. Therapy has enabled and taught me how to be a different person. My analytic training, which included five years of analysis, three times a week, has guided me to look deep inside myself, giving me the road map to my unconscious. Studying theorists like Freud, Klein, Winnicott, and others gave me the tools to allow myself to explore my inner self in a way I would not have been able to do otherwise.

Although I trained as a psychoanalyst, there were reasons why I never became one. I felt I was not smart enough to actually get my certification. I did not believe I would be able to get a client to come in three times a week for a long period of time and most, if not all, of my clients went through their insurance. Insurance would never pay for treatment that often.

The residual, old, bad message that was instilled in me by my parents never seemed to leave me. The message that I was never good enough or smart enough. It was the reason why I never pursued my analytic certification.

With that being said, analysis made me a better therapist. I was able to analyze my own clients on a much deeper level. If one can understand themselves, it enables them, on some level, to be able to approach understanding someone else. My husband always said the following to me: "You were able to give to your clients what you never got from your parents, and by giving to your clients, you were also giving to yourself."

This is not something that easily resonates with me. Despite all my therapy, a feeling of unworthiness continues to linger within me from my childhood. Whenever clients would praise me and tell me I was the best therapist they ever had, I countered that by saying: "It wasn't me, it was you that made the change. I was just the medium that allowed for that change to occur in you. This would not have happened if you weren't motivated toward change, I just showed you the map to which road you could take to being emotionally healthy." I am quite aware that I was the "good enough mother" to many of my clients and have helped many people. However, I never felt that "giving" to someone else was also "giving" to myself. I struggle with that concept and have difficulty accepting it.

It is still difficult for me to accept a compliment even today, but I no longer dispute the validity of the compliment. I thank them, take it in, and process it later on. I reject the idea that people are "just saying" things to be nice. I believe they are telling me the truth. It's just hard to recognize and accept positive feedback. It's hard to accept that I did something noteworthy. However, all of what I just described has enabled me to understand, relate, and empathize with my clients. This was my resilience. I cannot change my past, but I was able to change my future and change my perception of how I see the world and evaluate friendships. I was able to utilize my childhood experiences in order to help others, especially when it came to setting boundaries.

My resilience was a combination of forces coming together, such as survival, genetics, therapy, and education.

Survival: I had to learn how to read people at an early age; for example, my mother, to avoid punishment. I realize now that if I was not able to be as perceptive as I was, especially with my mother, I could have been dragged into very bad situations. Additionally, my need to be loved, wanted, and needed could have easily set me up for drug use and possibly criminal behavior. Recruiters for gangs and cults are tuned in to those who want to belong and feel lost, and I was a perfect candidate for joining such a group. Somehow, deep inside of me, I probably knew that the consequences were more frightening than being unwanted. I somehow had the strength to rely on myself, my self-reliance, resilience, without realizing it.

Genetics: My paternal grandparents immigrated to the United States in the early 1920s, and shortly after they had children, my grandfather died. The courage and strength my grandmother possessed deep within herself allowed her to raise three children and work outside the home. Women working outside the home back then was quite unusual. My grandmother persevered, found her inner strength, and was able to survive extremely difficult times. I believe that same tenacity was something that was generously passed down to me, something I inherited, and something my siblings did not.

I like to think my education and therapy go hand in hand. Even though my introduction to therapy was not my idea, I found the value in it. It was my own therapy that guided me toward becoming a therapist. I, the client, was the engine in therapy and the therapist was the gas pump that propelled me forward into a healthier life.

My post-graduate work at the analytic institute also had a big impact on my life. All the literature that I was required to read was dense and difficult. However, it was the master plan, the blueprint that allowed me to understand my mother's psyche and gave me insight into my own life, giving me an understanding of who I really am. I am going to assume that most of the other candidates in the program were possibly relating the readings to their clients. I was relating the readings to myself and my life.

I always believed communication to be key to a good relationship. If you truly understand and empathize with what the other person is going through, most issues could be resolved. However, if there is no communication, if a person is unable to allow themselves to be vulnerable and express their thoughts and feelings, nothing will be resolved.

Here is an example. Every morning, the first thing I do when I get up is drag myself into the kitchen and turn on the coffeemaker. I have my two cups of coffee a day over the course of forty-five minutes. Prior to retiring, my husband and I would be in the kitchen together and I would take the coffee spoon from the counter and put the spoon in the sink. Since my husband would be washing the dishes with the dish sponge, the coffee spoon's drippings would remain on the counter. The moment he finished with the sponge, I would immediately grab it and wipe the coffee stain from the counter. Marshall started getting upset with me saying, "What's the matter, I'm not doing it fast enough for you?" This happened a few times and it is unlike him to get upset. I knew the reason for my behavior. Living with my mother, everything had to be done immediately. Everything had to be clean, immaculate, and sterile, otherwise, there would be hell to pay. I finally said to Marshall, "Why are you getting so upset by my wiping the counter?" He said, "I feel like I'm not doing it quick enough for you." I realized the trigger for him was his ex, it was his own transference. For Marshall, if he did not get his ex her morning coffee fast enough, he would get yelled at, and for me, if I did not clean up my mess fast enough, I would get yelled at.

At this point, we were able to empathize with each other; we had an understanding where we were both coming from. From that point on, the issue was resolved and there was no more issue. If the counter was dirty, I knew he would do it, and it was not a matter of contention between us. This may sound trivial, but I believe most couples argue about trivial things. There is meaning behind everything we do. When I was in analysis, my analyst would question why I "sighed" when I did at any particular moment. That question served as an "intervention" that allowed for an exploration of some additional unconscious material within the analytic situation. It invariably uncovered a new insight and understanding for me. My own analysis taught me to be a much better therapist. It taught me to tune into a person's movements, facial expressions, and nonverbal communication to the extent that I would never have known to do otherwise.

Chapter 43

MY DREAM CAME TRUE

The day I finished setting up my very first office and hung up my diploma, I sat there and cried. Tears of happiness. In my head, this wasn't supposed to happen to me. My dream was not meant to come true. The odds were against me; however, I was finally surrounded by positive people, people who believed in me and supported me, like my therapist and my husband.

I had worked very hard to get where I was with no help from anyone. I depended on myself. I persevered. I never gave up. I worked very long hours every day and I enjoyed making money. But it was not about the money. My career was gratifying. It gave me pleasure. I was helping people.

Many of my clients have told me they had been through many different therapists before they found me. They liked the way I interacted and the fact that I didn't just sit there silent. This is not a criticism of other therapists. Everyone has their own style that works for them and their clients. My approach was interactive and many of my clients have admired my forthcomingness and my bluntness. I allowed them to see me as a real person and that enabled them to be comfortable, which encouraged them to talk more freely.

They would say, "You always hold me accountable." Which I did. There was no bullshit in my office coming out of my mouth. Some clients would say, "You have to say nice things to me, you're a therapist." For me that was not true; I believe giving a client a false sense of hope only sets them up for failure. However, if I felt a client was going down an unhealthy path, I would explore that with the client in a manner such that they were able to see for themselves and admit that their idea was not a good idea.

One's past never leaves one. The residuals can unconsciously influence the decisions we make. There are obvious reasons, which were not obvious before, why I wanted to go into private practice and not work at an agency. Being controlled by a supervisor, having to be restricted by state inspections, having to be beholden to higher-ups, and having to ask for time off—whether it be sick time, personal time, or vacation—was intolerable for me. I wanted to be able to call the shots. I did not want anyone looking over my shoulder. I did not want to have to answer to anyone, even though occasionally I had to answer to insurance companies. I was willing to compromise on that front. After all, there were some things I had to be realistic about.

Most of my colleagues did not take insurance and if they did, they were out of network. I decided to be an in-network provider for two reasons: first, I didn't want to forget where I came from, a blue-collar family. Second, being credentialed with insurance companies meant they did all the marketing for my practice because they referred clients to me. I was also on Psychology Today online directory of therapists from which I received many new clients. And once the Affordable Care Act was established, mental health was considered parity, which meant it was treated exactly like any other doctor's appointment. There was no more begging and justifying with the insurance company about why a person needed to be in treatment.

In 2008, when the economy crashed, my practice never suffered. My colleagues' practices slowed down because some people were unable to pay out of pocket. However, my practice flourished. Dealing with insurance companies eliminated any anxiety I had about getting new clients. New clients always presented themselves and occasionally I had to turn people away.

Months before my husband and I decided to move to the beach full-time, I had to set up a practice close to where I would be living. Surprisingly enough, I was not as anxious about doing this as one would think. I felt that I had done it before and I could surely do it again. Thinking about this now, I suspect this was my resilience kicking in.

The other interesting piece of this was I was used to seeing teenagers, and not many therapists in Central Jersey wanted to treat teens. In addition, they did not want to work with couples. Therefore, I filled a need.

I sublet an office from a colleague for a few months until I had about ten clients, which afforded me the opportunity to rent an office of my own. Unfortunately, finding an office was more difficult than I had anticipated. I had few options based on what I could afford. The first office I rented was a big old house, which became a bit eerie at night when I was the only one in the building. It was also not ideal mainly because there was no private waiting room. I had to share the waiting room with two other therapists.

I stayed there for a few years until one day a therapist down the hall had a client who brought a dog in that was not on a leash. My office door was open, and the dog decided to stroll into my office without its owner. I do not do pet therapy! I am allergic to animals, all sorts of animals. I spoke to the therapist who was not understanding about my situation. This was basically the "match in the powder barrel." I had not been comfortable in my office since I signed the lease feeling that the people who occupied the bottom floor were arrogant. My rent was fairly cheap, but I guess if you "pay for bananas, you get monkeys."

I had about four months more on my lease, but I had to get out. I looked around online and then called my friend Dan, who had sold us the condo, and asked for his help. Even though he was not into the leasing side of real estate, he put me in touch with someone who had office space. It was the perfect space for me on many levels. It had a kitchenette in the waiting room, it was bright and airy, the bathroom was modern and well-kept. But the most important amenity was how secure it was. No one could get onto the floor unless I buzzed them in. The rent was double what I was paying in the old place, but I knew I would feel safe at night being alone with my clients.

I told my landlord at the old office the issue and worked it out that I would pay off the rest of my lease and would be leaving almost immediately. I loved my new place and so did my clients.

Chapter 44

RETIREMENT

I spent several years in my new office with very few issues. My landlord was extremely nice and accommodating. I was content and had no plans to retire. In 2019, my financial guy needed a tentative retirement date in order to calculate and make sure Marshall and I would be financially prepared for when that day would come. I gave him a tentative year as to when this would happen. However, retirement was not something I was ready to do. I always said when insurance companies start to become problematic again, that is when I will retire. And that is exactly what happened. I found myself spending more time on the phone trying to collect money from them. Since I've "been there and done that," that was something I did not want to revisit.

However, on Friday, March 13, 2020, life as we knew it changed drastically. COVID was rampant. Marshall and I were afraid to leave the house, afraid to touch anything and anyone. We had scheduled our annual vacation to Antigua, and on that Friday, the day before we were to leave, we canceled our trip. I spent the entire week on the phone with insurance companies to figure out the new coding, since our sessions were now going to be telehealth. I will say the insurance companies worked well with the providers, as co-pays were waived for several months. But working from home was not ideal. I did my sessions in the bedroom and Marshall did his sessions in the dining room. The "traffic" in the kitchen became unbearable at times. His practice doubled and mine increased also. We made and saved an incredible amount of money since we were not going anywhere and not buying anything.

We worked from home for eighteen months, and I got to a point where I could not do it anymore and had to get out of the house. I went back to the office, just for a change of scenery, but still doing telehealth. We were fully vaccinated and venturing out of the house more. Being vaccinated meant I was able to see my grandkids again. Emotionally, I felt much better. Previously, before being vaccinated, it was too much of a risk to be with my kids and grandkids, not only for them but especially for my husband, who has a heart condition. Life had changed drastically and not for the better.

Retirement started to look better and better. My husband and I are physically and mentally in good shape, and with a family history of Alzheimer's, I decided it was best to retire while we were healthy and could enjoy ourselves. We enjoy traveling and can afford to do so.

Originally, we decided on a date of December 2022, but that date kept changing for many reasons. We had to close two offices, my stepson was getting married, and we decided to treat ourselves to a three-week vacation. With my stepson getting married and with COVID looming in the forefront of our minds, we needed time to insulate ourselves between coming home from vacation and attending the wedding. We needed to make sure we were healthy.

We retired at the end of September 2022 and closed my husband's office within two days. Two weeks after that we went on our vacation, returned, and had two weeks to isolate in the event we might have contracted COVID. We then went to the wedding and closed my office at the beginning of December.

The most difficult part of retiring was letting my clients know that in about six months our sessions would be ending. I expected clients to jump ship and leave prematurely. But that did not happen. I realized how connected they were to me and how important I was to them. This was hard for me to metabolize because I never felt important to anyone. But I was able to accept this compliment with both spoken and unspoken words. The unspoken words were their connection to me. They left the practice when I left the practice and not a moment sooner.

At the time I closed my practice, many of my clients had been with me for several years. It was just as hard for me as it was for them, and I am not sure they realized it. At the time I retired, some of my clients were in personal despair and trauma and I was unable to see them through their turmoil. The hardest part is I will never know the end of their story. It is equivalent of walking out in the middle of a movie, with no way of knowing how it ends. I think about my clients frequently.

Since I've been retired, my anxiety has been at an all-time low. There is no stress and nothing to worry about. I am not the kind of person who needs to be busy all the time. I enjoy doing nothing. The best part of my day is drinking my morning coffee in bed. My husband and I always seem to be busy, not really doing much of anything, but always seem to be doing something. Exactly what that "something" might be is anyone's guess.

For some couples, retirement is a big adjustment; an adjustment to being with your spouse all day, every day. Marshall and I never had to adjust to being with each other on that level. Marshall and I were best friends before we got married. We always enjoyed each other's company. We do have our moments, which are far and few between. We managed to figure out this "marriage" thing a long time ago.

Chapter 45

MY LIFE TODAY

As I reflect back on my life, I question whether I would have emotionally survived if I did not have this "fuck you" defense mechanism. Childhood defense mechanisms usually work against people once they mature. My "fuck you" attitude, from my perspective, has prevented me from feeling emotionally annihilated. It has been my way of surviving. I believe, I feel, my rebellion has prevented me from being swallowed up, consumed, and completely absorbed by my mother. Therapy has enlightened me, changed me, changed my perspective on life and on myself. I still have that "fuck you" attitude, but the premise behind it is different. I consciously choose not to deal with bullshit, which is different from not dealing with it as a way of surviving.

When I think about my relationship with June, which started before I had any therapy, it occurred to me that this was a relationship that should have never happened, as, previously, I only gravitated toward people who were like my mother. There had to be something deeply unconscious within me that pulled me toward her, as she was the most unlikely candidate for a friend. There was something within me, something that I was so oblivious to, that allowed me to

Diane Harth

continue my friendship with her. Back then, almost everyone in my life was dysfunctional, and almost everyone in my life was like my mother.

As messed up as I was back then, I am not sure how but I can honestly say I did a good job with my kids. They are hard-working, independent, educated adults. But what I am most impressed about with my kids is what great parents they are to their kids. Bernadette recently said this to me. "I am a better parent than you, and you were a better parent than your mother, and my kids will be better parents to their kids." I learned from my mother's mistakes and my kids learned from my mistakes. The only regret I have with myself as a parent was my lack of energy. I see my kids as having so much more energy as they are so involved with their kids. Both Bernadette and Jarret and their spouses work full-time jobs, and they still have all this energy to be at all their children's activities. I was always tired, and I wonder if it was because I did most of everything alone with the kids, along with keeping house. I also wonder if my Hashimoto's disease was always there and not diagnosed till later on in life. I am impressed with how my children parent with respect to the love and support they give to their children.

One of the most important changes that has occurred in my life is the decrease in anxiety. Therapy has helped considerably in this respect. I have learned how to identify the triggers that increase my anxiety and deal with them in very positive and appropriate ways. I have been able to identify my transference and recognize when someone is behaving like my mother or that something that I am experiencing is making me feel oppressed. Therapy has taught me to objectively look at a situation that creates discomfort and not become defensive. It taught me to not be impulsive, as I can now take the time to think through situations before I act. Therapy, along with my husband, taught me patience. When I started to go to therapy, I just wanted someone to listen to me. It never occurred to me that I needed to change anything about myself. I was not self-aware at that time. I did not have an observing ego, meaning I was not able to look at myself objectively. As I look back, I was forced to be patient because therapy takes time. Patience is a requirement for the process of therapy to succeed. Therapy taught me how to be patient with other things in my life. Therapy cannot be rushed. Therapy takes time. It is not a quick fix. Because of the nature of therapy, my development of patience was camouflaged by the treatment. My patience and my resilience were the ingredients for the recipe for my good mental health.

However, along with therapy, the other most important event in my life was meeting my husband, Marshall. My life has changed dramatically since he came into my life. He became my best friend, my lover, my support system. I would take a bullet for him and give him a kidney (I say I would give him a kidney because I probably wouldn't be a match for him due to blood type). Marshall calms me. He is my voice of reason. Ironically, *everything* always works out for him, regardless of the situation. He listens to me without criticism. He is warm and thoughtful and most of all, he can manage my anxiety. I feel fortunate to have crossed paths with him. I am the happiest I have ever been in my life.

Therapy has changed my life, and no matter how much therapy one has, there is still another layer to peel back and look at the rawness behind that layer. One needs to pick at that rawness slowly until it bleeds, scabs, and heals. Change occurs when one is able to accept who they are, allow themselves to be vulnerable, shift their perceptions, and see themselves in a different light. My life was a game of musical chairs; never having a seat at the table. My new life consists of everyone having a seat at the table, with no shortage of chairs.

My father was only as happy as the saddest family member and my mother was the saddest. I believe if my mother observed my father being happy, she would then have to look at herself and question why she was so unhappy. And maybe it extends past my dad. I highly doubt she was able to tolerate anyone being happy.

With respect to my mother, I can acknowledge that she was a victim of her times—the Great Depression. Whatever she had gone through growing up, she internalized. She never allowed herself to expel the toxin that lay dormant deep inside her well of despair. That well was deep, dark, and cold. It was empty. She wouldn't allow herself to hear her childhood echoing in this chamber. She refused to allow herself to grab onto the rope that dangled in front of her, to be pulled out of the hollowness she experienced in her life. Her fear was encapsulated by bricks, preventing her from feeling any happiness. She was unable, or refused, to chip away and dismantle the bricks. My mother was repeatedly reinforced by her compulsion to control everything in her life, believing it was working, as it kept her own anxiety at bay. I wish I knew what else she struggled with in her life, as I know almost nothing about her life. I would've been more understanding of why she did the things she did, not only to me but to our family. If she had been more open about her life, I might have been more compassionate, understanding, and empathetic. It saddens me to think that my mother's life was such a mystery.

Writing has become a revelation for me. Writing allowed me to reflect deeply on my past, which enabled me to understand myself better. I realized the true reason I became a therapist. This realization was buried deep in the depths of my soul, deep in the darkness of the abyss of my unconscious mind. I was unaware of how remote the deprivation existed within me. The void and lack of emotional communication in my family of origin was a slow death for me. Somehow this deprivation, unconsciously, gave me the strength to change my life around. I became a therapist because of my need to connect to others, as therapy is the most intimate situation anyone will ever experience. Connection is what allows people to survive.

I will admit that I am no longer angry. But I am pained by my experience. My mother made me the person I am today and I have very mixed emotions about that. I am able to feel empathy for her and whatever childhood experiences made her who she was. I do, however, still hold her responsible for how she treated me. As I said to her when she was lying in her coffin, "It didn't have to be this way."

I am happy with who I am and accept my imperfections along with my virtues and my integrities. I feel fortunate that I was able to change my life around and I did this all on my own. My own decision, my own strength, and my own resilience. I survived!

AFTERTHOUGHTS

If only things were different. What would my life have been like if my mother had been more compassionate, loving, and understanding? If she was open to listening to what I had to say; if she was only more emotional. If she was empathic. What would my life have been like if she had allowed me to have and explore my dreams? What if she taught me right from wrong and not just wrong? Would I have become the person I am today? Would I have been so driven to prove myself, not only to the outside world but to myself? I wonder if I could have achieved what I have achieved or would I have felt it was less important to be so motivated and driven? Would I have always second-guessed myself and beat myself up on my every action, move, word, and thought? Would I have continued to second-guess myself in the face of success? Would I have continued to deny the good that lies within me? Would I have still struggled to reject the negative image they had of me?

My mother molded me into who I am today; my tenacity, my strength, my stubbornness, and my fearlessness to defend myself and never walk away from an argument. Because of my mother, I've become a strong, productive woman who is able to accomplish any goal I set for myself.

I am able to rely on myself. Most of the time I depend only on myself because if I succeed at my goals, I know I've done it on my own, and if I fail, it is also on me. But I am proud of all my failures and successes because I learned valuable life skills from both.

In a very twisted way and against everything the Italian culture stood for back then, my mother groomed me to be a BITCH—"being in total control of herself."

IF ONLY she…

ACKNOWLEDGMENTS

First and foremost, I would like to thank Luminare Press for making it possible for me to publish my memoir into an actual book. I could not have done this without your help and expertise. I appreciate your efficiency and follow-up without my having to initiate contact. Special thanks to Christine Scaduto, Kim Harper-Kennedy, Melissa Thomas, Sallie Vandagrift, Jerry Fingal, Luigi Ricco and Caitlin McCrum.

To Bernadette and Jarret; I admire both of you for your parenting skills. Parenting is the hardest job in the world. You have both learned from your own childhoods how to be better parents from the previous generations.

I would like to thank Noreen Bruns for reading the early version of my memoir and giving me feedback. I would also like to thank Charley Bruns for his overwhelming support, guidance, and encouragement. Charley was my fan club who continually stood by me every step of the way, especially when I was ready to give up. Charley assisted me through very difficult times, making this journey easier for me to achieve. He showed me the path to publishing my book. Thank you from the bottom of my heart.

To my best and longtime friend, June Bittel. How lucky

am I to have met such a caring, wonderful person who always accepted me for who I am. You are one of the most trustworthy people I have ever come across. You have always stuck with me through very difficult times and never left my side. I love you. Thank you for coming into my life.

Dr. D. You have changed my life in ways that go beyond a few sentences. Your patience with me was positively astounding. The imprint you made in my life is indelible. I owe my career choice to you along with an understanding of who I am.

Thank you.

Dr. Ben Pinker. Thank you for all your clinical input on the manuscript and the amount of time spent analyzing not only me but also my dysfunctional family. Your analysis validated my feelings and also gave me a better understanding of dynamics that engulfed me for most of my life.

I would like to thank Dr. Donna Crawley for offering to copy edit my manuscript. I realize this was a major undertaking and I truly appreciate the time you spent on it.

To my friend N.A., you have stated how much my book helped you. However, you have also made me feel that my book was worth writing. Thank you for all our conversations.

Special thanks to Nikole Batista for her critique. Nikole, I admire how you were able to make suggestions on how I can improve my book in an unbiased manner. Thank you.

Thank you, David Harth for collaborating with me and your dad on the design of the cover of my book. I always appreciate your input.

Special thanks to Barbara Shweky and Nan Simon,

who belong to my husband's book club, for their input and suggestions on how to improve my book. It is greatly appreciated.

To my friends Dan Wright and Darlene Aikman, who read the very first rough draft. Both of your comments were taken very seriously, which led me to rethink about how to write a memoir.

To Scott Perotti, my personal trainer, who has taught me endurance, regardless of the pain, which enabled me to, at times, suffer through writing my book. Most importantly, your comments and suggestions were well received and greatly appreciated.

To Dr. Tom Johnson, whom I always looked up to and admired. Thank you for spending time with me on how to proceed with my book and guiding me on the ins and outs of publishing my book.

To Ashley Harvey, as much as you have told me how my book resonated with you, your comments have also done the same for me. I thank you for taking the time out of your busy schedule to read my memoir.

And last of all, Marshall. I don't know what road my life would be on if our paths had not crossed. You are my shining light who guides me on a constant path of optimism. I don't believe I would have been a successful therapist or had a successful private practice if it wasn't for your constant encouragement. I don't know if I would have finished the book when my old computer crashed and I lost a hundred pages of the manuscript and then spent four days rewriting it from the hard copy. You read every "freakin" word of the manuscript several times, such that you can almost quote it verbatim. You are my knight in shining armor who is constantly by my side, regardless of the situation. Thank you for coming into my life. I love you with all my heart.

Made in the USA
Columbia, SC
08 December 2024

48770053R00181